Great Secrets, Mysteries, And Revelations Of The Holy Bible

By
Dr. Antwane Duane Rosemane

Preface 1
Introduction

All glory to ELOHIM (GOD). In accordance with and agreement to the Messiah (Christ), and Revelation 19:10, the Spirit of YHWH ELOHIM and of prophecy was upon me heavily as the HOLY SPIRIT moved me to write this Book of Revelation of ELOHIM's Word and Truth. The main reason for the production of this book is to reveal things to the saints that have been hidden for centuries, and to prepare the Bride (the Church) for her husband (Christ). For Christ Himself revealed to me that He will be returning "very soon" for His people. Amen.

I would like to note the meaning of my Church's and Religion's Logo Ensign Symbol, which is a Heart with a Cross in its center and a Lightning Bolt striking it. This symbolizes the Great LOVE of ELOHIM, the Great Sacrifice of Christ, and the Great Power of the HOLY SPIRIT in the lives of believers. As the Founder and President of The Bride of Christ Ministries and The UP Religion, and a Man of ELOHIM, I am called, chosen, Anointed, and appointed (ordained) to win souls into the Kingdom of Heaven by fulfilling the Great Commission found in St. Matthew 28:18-20 and St. Mark 16:15-18. Amen.

My prayer, according to St. James 5:16, is that each reader of this book finds not my words, but the Words of YHWH ELOHIM spoken and written through me, as the MOST HIGH EL continues using me as HIS vessel, tool, and instrument to accomplish HIS will; to edify the saints, and to encourage HIS people and Church with these insightful Revelations and Truths, enlightening and illuminating your spirit with the wisdom, understanding, and knowledge found in the pages hereafter. May the great and good GOD YAHWEH bless you, your loved ones, and all that you possess. In the Name of King JESUS Christ, the Nazarene, YAHUSHUA, YESHUA, IMMANU'EL the Messiah. Amen and Amen. Again, all glory be to the MOST HIGH ELOHIM, the LIVING ELOHIM, the only ELOHIM: I AM THAT I AM (YHWH). Amen and Shalom!

Preface 2
Acknowledgements

First and foremost, I acknowledge and glorify my FATHER in heaven, the MOST HIGH EL SHADDAI, and His Son, JESUS CHRIST (YAHUSHUA MESSIAH), and the HOLY SPIRIT (RUACH HA KODESH), that HE is ONE. See 1st John 5:7(KJV). Amen.

Next, I acknowledge and thank all of the Heavenly Hosts, my spiritual family, my brothers and sisters in Christ(the Saints).I acknowledge my gratefulness unto JEHOVAH ELOHIM for mine GOD~ fearing children whom HE has given me, Tabetha (daughter) and Nakomi (granddaughter) both are still learning how to perfect the fear of The LORD MOST HIGH ELOHIM(The LORD's will be done with them in Mercy)for besides my Heavenly Family(HOLY SPIRIT, etc.), my daughters are my greatest inspiration: Be blessed in Christ the Messiah. Amen. I would like to thank Ms. Natasha for welcoming me into her home when I had no place to go. May YAH bless you with Shalom and Mercy according to HIS will for that, in the Mighty name of JESUS. Amen.

Also, I thank and bless my "spiritual" sons and daughters(children) whom I've adopted in the faith, brethren Angel, T.K.; all of my Elders and my personal Mentors bro. Emmanuel, and bro.Peter; and I also bless all of mine Disciples in Christ. Amen. All those who were there for me when I needed you most, may YHWH(YAHWEH) continue to bless you and the Family and keep you safe. Amen.

I would like to thank the CREATOR and MAKER of all things, the CREATOR of my being, who made me and shaped me, the MOST HIGH ELOHIM, for helping me throughout my life, for Being the only Father I have ever known and the only FATHER I have ever needed. To my earthly family(as distinct from my Spiritual) and to all who have supported me, thank you so much. I am grateful for everything! May YAHWEH continue to be merciful unto you in hopes that you repent and receive the Gift of EL. before it's too late! Amen.

My helpers and sisters and daughters in the Faith(Women of GOD/Women of Faith) Tina, Trina, Keya, Lala, Mrs. Marilyn, Mrs. Deborah, Ms. Sharon, Mrs. Yolette, Ms. Janiyah King, and again, my baby Tabetha Diamond. Amen LOVE.

Finally, I would like to thank EL SHADDAI for the many blessings HE has bestowed upon me, for my journey, and for the wisdom I have gained. May YAHWEH continue to guide me and provide me with the strength I need. For I can do all things through HIS Son, mine Big Brother YAHUSHUA IMMAN'U-EL Christ Messiah. Blessings to you all! I am thankful to YHWH for your LOVE, wisdom, and understanding, and my prayer is that My people no longer perish for lack of Wisdom. In the Name of Christ. May He continue to guide you and bless you all. Amen.

Table of Contents

Chapter 1:
Great Facts of The Holy Bible

Note: Some of these statistics may vary from source to source or Versions of The Holy Scriptures. The reader is encouraged to check them personally.

1. The Holy Bible was written by some forty holy men of ELOHIM over a period of about 1,600 years (1,500 BC-100 AD). See 2 Peter 1:20-:21 + 1 Corinthians 2:13 + 2 Timothy 3:16-17. ELOHIM Himself wrote a portion (The Ten Commandments) with His own Finger. See Exodus 31:18.

2. The system of Chapters was introduced in 1238 AD by Cardinal Hugo de S. caro, while verse notations were added in 1551 by Robertus Stephanus, after the advent of printing.

3. The Holy Bible can be read aloud in 70 hours, silent reading is faster. Thus, one can read through the whole Bible five to six times per year at an hour a day.

4. There are 8,674 different Hebrew words in the Hebrew Old Testament(Tanakh); there are 5,624 different Greek words in the New Testament(B'rit Hadashah); and 12,143 different English words in the entire King James Bible.

5. Studies reveal that the number of new Bibles that are sold, given away, or otherwise distributed in the United States are approximately 168,000 per day.

6. Total number of Books in the Authorized Holy Bible:66; Chapters: 1,189; Verses: 31,101; Words: 783,137; letters: 3,566,480; longest name: Mahershalalhashbaz (18 letters) (Isaiah 8:1); longest

Verse: Esther 8:9 (90 words); shortest Verse: St. John 11:35 (two words: "JESUS wept"); longest Chapter: Psalms 119 (176 Verses); shortest Chapter(by number of words): Psalm 117; middle Books: Micah and Nahum; middle Verse: Psalm 118:8; middle Chapter: Psalm 117; longest Book: Psalms (150 Chapters); shortest Book(by number of words): 3rd John; number of times the Name or Title "GOD" or "ELOHIM" appears: 3,915; number of times the Title or Name "YHWH" or "LORD" appears: 6,751; total number of Authors of the Books of The Holy Bible:40.

7. Old Testament Statistics:

Number of Books: 39; Chapters:929; Verses:23,114; Words: 602,585; letters: 2,278,100; middle Book: Proverbs; middle Chapter: Ezra 2; middle Verse: 2 Chronicles 20;17,18; shortest Book: Obadiah; shortest Verse: 1 Chronicles 1:25; longest Verse: Esther 8:9; longest Book: Psalms; longest Chapter: Psalm 119.

8. New Testament Statistics:

Number of Books: 27; Chapters: 260; Verses: 7,957; Words: 180,552; letters: 838,380; middle Book: 2 Thessalonians; middle Chapters: Romans 13,14; middle Verse: Acts 27:17; shortest Book: 3 John; shortest Verse: St. John 11:35; longest Book: St, Luke; longest Chapter: St. Luke 1; longest Verse: Revelation 20:4.

9. The Number of Chapters in each Book:

(1) Genesis 50

(2) Exodus 40

(3) Leviticus 27

(4) Numbers 36

(5) Deuteronomy 34

(6) Joshua 24

(7) Judges 21

(8) Ruth 4

(9) 1 Samuel 31

(10) 2 Samuel 24

(11) 1 Kings 22

(12) 2 Kings 25

(13) 1 Chronicles 29

(14) 2 Chronicles 36

(15) Ezra 10

(16) Nehemiah 13

(17) Esther 10

(18) Job 42

(19) Psalms 150

(20) Proverbs 31

(21) Ecclesiastes 12

(22) Songs Of Solomon 8

(23) Isaiah 66

(24) Jeremiah 52

(25) Lamentations 5

(26) Ezekiel 48

(27) Daniel 12

(28) Hosea 14

(29) Joel 3

(30) Amos 9

(31) Obadiah 1

(32) Jonah 4

(33) Micah 7

(34) Nahum 3

(35) Habakkuk 3

(36) Zephaniah 3

(37) Haggai 2

(38) Zechariah 14

(39) Malachi 4

(40) St. Matthew 28

(41) St. Mark 16

(42) St. Luke 24

(43) St. John 21

(44) Acts 28

(45) Romans 16

(46) 1 Corinthians 16

(47) 2 Corinthians 13

(48) Galatians 6

(49) Ephesians 6

(50) Philippians 4

(51) Colossians 4

(52) 1 Thessalonians 5

(53) 2 Thessalonians 3

(54) 1 Timothy 6

(55) 2 Timothy 4

(56) Titus 3

(57) Philemon 1

(58) Hebrews 13

(59) St. James 5

(60) 1 Peter 5

(61) 2 Peter 3

(62) 1 John 5

(63) 2 John 1

(64) 3 John 1

(65) St. Jude 1

(66) Revelation 22.

10. Christ the Messiah (which means "The Anointed One") always existed and always will; He was mentioned even in the Old Testament. See Exodus 17:6 + 1 Corinthians 10:4 + Numbers 20:8-11. Furthermore, majority of the prophecies, even from the Garden of Eden, were of Christ and His coming in the flesh: from "The Seed" of Adam and Eve, to "The Word becoming flesh and dwelling among us." Amen.

Chapter 2:
Great Truths of The Holy Bible.

(See St. John 8:32 +14:6 + 16:13-15)

1.Abraham is the father of faith. Thus, whoever has faith is a child of Abraham. See Galatians 3:7-9 (KJV) "Know ye therefore that they which are of faith, the same are the children of Abraham.8. And the Scripture, foreseeing that ELOHIM would justify the heathen through faith, preached before the Gospel unto Abraham, saying, In thee shall all nations be blessed.9. So then they which be of faith are blessed with faithful Abraham." Amen.

2.Although Abraham, Isaac, and Ya'aqob(Jacob), and even Yahudah(Judah) have many sons and daughters, yet when you become One with Christ the Messiah in His Body, you become a new creation(creature), and become a member of His Family. And as such, we have only One FATHER(GOD-which is in heaven), and One Rabbi/Teacher/Master(Christ-the Son of GOD). See 2 Corinthians 5:17(KJV) "Therefore if any man be in Christ, he is a new creature: old things are passed away; behold, all things are become new." Amen. See also St. Matthew 23:8-10(KJV) "But be not ye called Rabbi: for One is your Master, even Christ; and all ye are brethren.9. And call no man your father upon the earth: for One is your Father, which is in heaven.10. Neither be ye called masters: for One is your Master, even Christ." Amen.

From these Holy Scriptures we perceive both the blasphemy and the disobedience to call any human or anyone else besides

ELOHIM(GOD) your Father, and to call any human or anyone other than the Messiah Himself Master or Teacher or Rabbi. Amen.

3.Melchizedek is an eternal king and priest of the MOST HIGH EL: he has neither beginning nor end, and is "like the Son of ELOHIM", and to whom even Abraham(the friend of ELOHIM) paid tithes. See Hebrews 7:1-3(KJV) "For this Melchiz'edek, king of Salem, priest of the MOST HIGH ELOHIM, who met Abraham returning from the slaughter of the kings, and blessed him;2. to whom also Abraham gave a tenth part of all; first being by interpretation King of righteousness, and after that also King of Salem, which is, King of peace;3. without father, without mother, without descent, having neither beginning of days, nor end of life; but made like unto the Son of ELOHIM; abideth a priest continually." Amen. See also Hebrews 7:8-10. Amen.

Arguably, Melchizedek is perhaps the most mysterious person in the Bible, since many Verses in the Bible speaks about ELOHIM Himself, and His Son Christ, but only a very few of Melchizedek; hence, this is a more than welcome insight and revelation of him as the eternal Priest of the MOST HIGH EL SHADDAI. For he is "like unto the Son of ELOHIM", because only ELOHIM and His Son Messiah has no beginning(always existed). Amen.

4.Leah was Ya'aqob's(Jacob's) first wife because of trickery by Laban(Leah's father),son of Nahor. See Genesis 29:18-28. Verse 25 says, "So it came to pass in the morning, that behold, it was Leah. And he(Ya'aqob) said to Laban, 'What is this you have done to me? Was it not for Rachel that I served you? Why then have you deceived me?" Amen.

5.Ya'aqob served 7 years for Leah, then 7 years for Rachel, then an extra 6 to 7 years for Laban's flock. See Genesis 31:14. Amen.

6.Rachel was a Shepherdess. See Genesis 29:6,9. Amen.

7.Leah bore Ya'aqob his first four sons(Reuben, Simeon, Levi, Yahudah[Judah]); Rachel was barren at this time, but later in life ELOHIM answered her prayer and made her womb fruitful. See Genesis 29:31-35 + 30:22-24. Amen.

8.Ya'aqob's next four sons are: Dan (from Rachel's servant Bilhah-See Genesis 30:3-6) Naphtali (from Rachel's servant Bilhah- See Verses 7-8); Gad (from Leah's servant Zilpah- See Verses 9-11); and Asher (from Leah's servant Zilpah- See Verses 12-13). Amen.

9.Ya'aqob's last four sons are from both his wives, two from Leah, and the last two from Rachel. Leah bore him Yissaskar and Zebulun; and Rachel bore him Yoseph (Joseph) and his youngest son Benyamin (Benjamin). Rachel died while giving birth to Benyamin. See Genesis 35:16-19. Thus, that is the precise order of Ya'aqob's sons (from eldest to youngest). See Genesis 35: 22b-26. Also, Leah bore Ya'aqob a daughter name Dinah. However, her name is not mentioned as one of the 12 Tribes of Israel, because the Twelve Tribes are named after Jacob's twelve sons only. Amen.

10.ELOHIM reveals His Name as "EL SHADDAI" to Isreal in Genesis 35:11. EL SHADDAI means "ELOHIM ALMIGHTY" (GOD ALMIGHTY). Amen.

11.ELOHIM revealed another One of His Sacred Names to Moshey (Moses) in Exodus 3:14, "And ELOHIM said to Moses, 'I AM WHO I AM', or 'I AM THAT I AM'. And He said, 'Thus you shall say to the children of Israel, "I AM has sent me to you."'" Amen.

12.Again, in Verse 15 of the 3rd Chapter of Genesis, EL make known His two most Sacred Names that He is to be remembered by for eternity: "Moreover ELOHIM said to Moshae(Moses), 'Thus you shall say to the children of Israel: 'YHWH(YAHWEH in English) ELOHIM of your fathers, the ELOHIM of Abraham, the

ELOHIM of Isaac, and the ELOHIM of Ya'aqob, has sent me to you. This is My Name forever, and this is My memorial to all generations." Amen.

It shall be noted that Hebrew is the tongue and language that ELOHIM and His Son Christ chose to speak and have the Holy Scriptures written in. See also Acts 26:14. Thus in the Original Scriptures the LORD's Name (YHWH) was written or spoken, not the title "LORD" or "the LORD"; and ELOHIM or EL SHADDAI or ELOAH or EL, not the title "GOD" (or "God") or "GOD ALMIGHTY". "YHWH" is the "Tetragrammaton" Name of ELOHIM and is generally considered and accepted by most Scholars as His Most Sacred Personal Name, besides "ELOHIM", which is His first Name that He ever revealed to His children and creation at large, in the very first Verse of the Holy Bible: "In the beginning ELOHIM created the heaven(s) and the earth." See Genesis 1:1. Amen. Thus, His Sacred Personal Name "ELOHIM" is also His Most Sacred Name, and it means "The CREATOR GOD", "The Living GOD", "The MOST HIGH GOD", "The ANCIENT", "The ANCIENT ONE", and "The ANCIENT of Days". Amen.

GOD's Sacred Name "YHWH" is pronounced in Hebrew as "YOD HAY WAV HEY", and pronounced in English "YAHWEH". This Sacred Name of The MOST HIGH has two main meanings, one in relation to the FATHER: " I AM THAT I AM" or "I AM WHO I AM", meaning that the LORD GOD is all that He desires and choose to be, All-Powerful and above all. In theological terms this is called "OMNIPOTENT" (ALL POWERFUL), "OMNISCIENT" (ALL WISE and ALL KNOWING), and "OMNIPRESENT" (ALL PRESENT or PRESENT EVERYWHERE SIMUTANEOUSLY). The other meaning of this Most Sacred Name unequivocally refers to the Son of ELOHIM, because it means "Nails in Hands" or "the One whose Hands were Hammered with Nails". Clearly it was the

Son who was crucified on the tree (Cross) with nails in His Hands or wrist. This Name, along with the Sacred Names "IMMANUEL" or "EMMANUEL", which means "GOD with us" or "EL with us", "EL" means "GOD" in Hebrew, and "Christ" or "Messiah", which means "The ANOINTED ONE", shows most profoundly that JESUS is GOD or "ONE with GOD the FATHER". See also St. John 10:30, where YAHUSHUA(JESUS) said "I and My FATHER are ONE." See also the two Verses prior to that one where He is speaking about His and the FATHER's 'Hand'. Amen. Thus, "YHWH ELOHIM", which in English is interpreted "The LORD GOD" or "The LORD GOD MOST HIGH" or "LORD GOD ALMIGHTY", is indeed ELOHIMs Most Sacred Name. Furthermore, "ADONAI" also means "LORD" or "my LORD", and is used mostly by Orthodox and Messianic Jews. See Amos 4:13 "…The LORD GOD of hosts is His Name." Amen.

13"Baal" means "lord", and is not the true LORD GOD. ELOHIM does not like to be called "Baal" or "lord"(because He is not Baal and Baal is not Him) and He promises to "destroy permanently" all the "Baals" and remove their names from memory for eternity. Amen. See Judges 2:11-13 + Hosea 2:13,16-17. Amen.

14.Many argue about the precise order of importance of these three: "Wisdom, Understanding, Knowledge". While nearly everyone agree(myself included) that Wisdom is the greatest of these three(the Principal thing-See Proverb 4:7), it is often debated and not readily know which of the other two comes next in rank or importance. Of course it is beneficial and even necessary to have all three of the great qualities for a successful and productive life, but we are just comparing, say, for instance, if we had to choose in which order we prioritize the need and value of each. I, myself, used to always say: Wisdom, Knowledge, and Understanding, until I found in the Word the order in which ELOHIM says it: "Wisdom,

Understanding, and Knowledge". And His Way is always right! See Exodus 31:3. Amen. And actually I understand that this is the most correct and logical way or order, because it is like a ladder in which you climb up towards the MOST HIGH; these three qualities are like three steps: Knowledge is the first step up because you must receive whatever information first and become aware or "knowledgeable" of that information first, before you can perceive, comprehend, and understand that information. In other words, since knowledge is "knowing something" without the actual understanding or application of that knowledge, you must first simply receive the knowledge before the understanding or application of that knowledge can be discerned or utilized. For example, you may "know" something is hot, but you may not "understand" how it got hot, what makes it hot, or how it stays hot, or even how it can be cooled down. Or you may "know" 12x12=144 because someone may have simply "told" you that information, but you may not "understand" why or how is it 144. You may lack the greater understanding and wisdom of what makes 12x12=144, such as adding 12 times itself 12 times. So yes, the Understanding of something is a deeper and greater realm of Spiritual Intelligence than mere Knowledge, and Wisdom is greater and deeper than them both, because Wisdom encompasses(includes) both Knowledge and Understanding; and moreover, it is the utilization, practicality, and application of one's knowledge and understanding. Notwithstanding, we acknowledge that "Knowledge" is very important, so much so that ELOHIM proclaimed, "My people perish (or are destroyed) for lack of knowledge". See Hosea 4:6. Amen. This, quite sadly, shows that EL's people have not yet even climbed unto the first step towards reaching the FATHER. The hope in this is that YAHWEH said this about His people in the Tanakh (Old Testament). Hopefully our people are doing better with knowledge in this New Testament era. Amen.

15.Wisdom (the Spirit of Wisdom) resides in the "heart". See Exodus 31:6 + Proverbs 4:23. Amen.

16.The Ten Commandments are "perpetual" Laws (meaning they are to be obeyed forever), and the Holy Sabbath Day is actually "Saturday" (sat-your-day=rest), not Sunday, as many Christians believe. However, that is not to say that believers cannot go to Church and worship ELOHIM on Sunday too, because ELOHIM is worthy and should be worshipped "everyday"! Nonetheless, it does means that ELOHIM the CREATOR sanctified Saturday specifically as the Day of rest for His creation, which is to be hallowed above all other days and kept holy. See Isaiah 56:4-7 + Exodus 31:12-18; and for the complete Ten Commandments, See Exodus 20:1-17 + Deuteronomy 5:6-21; and to see that the Sabbath Day is specifically Saturday, See particularly Exodus 20:11(where ELOHIM rested the Seventh Day, hallowed it, and made it the Sabbath Day-for the correct first day of the American Calendar is Sunday. Thus, Saturday is the Seventh Day. Also See St. Matthew 28:1 where it confirms that after the Sabbath comes "the first day of the week". Furthermore, Easter is called "Easter Sunday", because it is the Day that JESUS rose: He was "in the heart of the Earth" three days (He died and went into the heart of the earth on Friday, and remained in there on Saturday-where He rested in the earth- and then arose on Sunday-the Day after Saturday(the Holy Sabbath)). See St. Matthew 28. Amen.

17.ELOHIM Himself wrote the Ten Commandments. Although He gave many Commandments to be written through His servants, the holy prophets(seers), He wrote The Ten Commandments with His own Finger. See Exodus 31:18; 32:16 + Deuteronomy 5:22. Amen.

18.The Holy Bible has been translated into over 1,200 different languages. Thus, we are approaching the prophecy of JESUS: "And this gospel of the kingdom shall be preached in all the world for a witness unto all nations; and then shall the end come." See St. Matthew 24:14. Amen. For the Word itself is getting around, but it is the lack of willing preachers(laborers), and the worldwide preaching of the Gospel that is prolonging the coming of the end. That is what Christ meant when He said, "the harvest truly is plentiful, but the laborers are few." See St. Matthew 9:37 + St. Luke 10:2. Amen.

19.Some words that occur only once in The Holy Bible: "eternity" (Isaiah 57:15); "reverend" (Psalm 111:9 KJV); "grandmother" (2 Timothy 1:5); "gnat" (St. Matthew 23:24); "boy" (Joel 3:3); "girl" (Joel 3:3). Amen.

20.Sometimes ELOHIM will change His Mind or relent. See Exodus 32:14. Amen.

21.No one can see ELOHIM's Face and live. See Exodus 33:20,23. Amen.

22.YHWH spoke to Moshay (Moses) Face-to-face. See Exodus 33:11. Amen.

23.YHWH ELOHIM Name is "Jealous". See Exodus 34:14. Amen. For YHWH ELOHIM is the only ONE who has a right to get or be jealous, for He created all and all. The CREATOR alone is worthy and deserving of worship, therefore if worship is given to anything or anyone else (the creatures or the created), He is rightfully so jealous. For Isreal and all Christians (the Church) are the Bride of the FATHER YHWH ELOHIM and HIS Christ, the Messiah. Thus, any infidelity on behalf of the bride causes the Husband to be jealous. See Hosea 2:16-20 + Ephesians 5:25-27 + 2 Corinthians 11:2 + Revelation 19:7-9; 21:2,9 + Proverbs 6:34-35. Amen.

24.Mosheh is one of three men in the Holy Bible that fasted 40 days and 40 nights (not eating nor drinking). Moreover, he did it twice. See Deuteronomy 9:9,18. The other two are YAHUSHUA Messiah (JESUS the Christ), and Elijah the Prophet. See St. Matthew 4:2 + 1 Kings 19:8. Amen.

25.ELOHIM(GOD) has a SOUL. See Leviticus 26:11. Amen.

26.The Book of "Jude" is really the Book of "Judah" ("Yahudah" in Hebrew). Amen.

27.The Hebrew name "Ya'aqob" (Jacob) is equivalent to "James" in English. Amen.

28.Yahudah (Judah) and his children (descendants) are Latin or "Spanish", as evidenced by the Spanish/Latin surname "Perez", Judah's fourth born son. See St. Matthew 1:3. Amen. It is widely believed that the now so-called "gang" of "Latin Kings" were not a gang at all originally, but initially an actual dynasty of literal "Latin Kings", or Kings with Latin (mixed) ancestry and descent (such as Puerto Ricans, Dominicans, Cubans, Mexicans, etc.), but the latter generations corrupted the purity of that dynasty/kingdom. Ironically, the Tribe of Judah is the line where the great Kings come from (King David, King Solomon, King JESUS, etc.). Amen.

29.When YAHWEH ELOHIM gave some of His Spirit to others besides Moshay, they prophesied too. See Numbers 11:17,25-29. Amen.

30.Moshay was the most humble/meek man on Earth in his day. See Numbers 12:3; EL spoke to him "Mouth to mouth" (plainly), and not in riddles. This is different than how EL spoke to His other Prophets. See Numbers 12:3,6-8. Amen.

31.YHWH is Israel's "Husband". See Hosea 2:16. Amen.

32.Moshey and his brother Aaron did not enter into the Promised Land because of the sin of rebellion (disobedience); for they disobeyed the Voice of YHWH when He Commanded them to "speak to" the rock, they (specifically Moses) "struck" the rock instead. See Numbers 20:8,11-12,24;27:13-14 + Deuteronomy 1:37;4:21;32:50-52. Amen. Aaron himself committed the sin of idolatry and caused the Israelites to commit the same, by making and worshipping a golden calf while Moshay was up on Mount Sinai 40 days and 40 nights communing with YAHWEH and receiving the Ten Commandments from Him. See Exodus 32:1-8. Amen.

33.YHWH must open your eyes(spiritual eyes) for you to see into the spiritual realm; then you will be able to perceive and see angels and spirits, etc. See Numbers 22:31 + 2 Kings 6:16-17. Amen.

34.Pinehas, son of Elazar, son of Aaron, has a permanent (everlasting) priesthood, because of his enthusiasm (zeal) for ELOHIM. See Numbers 25:10-13. Amen.

35.YHWH ELOHIM (The MOST HIGH GOD) is the Judge of gods. See Psalms 82 (spec. Verse 1) + Numbers 33:4b. He is the ELOHIM of gods (the GOD of gods): GOD ALMIGHTY "EL SHADDAI". See Psalms 136:2 and Revelation 4:8. Amen.

36.Israel first stepped foot into the Promised Land when they entered Elim, as evidenced by the Twelve springs of water (symbolizing a spring for each Tribe [Provision]); and also the Seventy palm trees (7 being one of ELOHIM's favorite numbers, and symbolizes completion, wholeness and perfection). Thus, these springs and trees were clear signs of YHWH's Provision and the Perfection of the Promised Land, a Land that floweth with milk and honey. See Numbers 33:9. Amen.

37. YAHWEH ELOHIM is He who give peoples their lands. See Deuteronomy 2:4-19. And although YAHWEH hated Esau, He still gave him land. See spec. Verse 5 of Deuteronomy 2 + Malachi 1:2-3. Amen.

38. ELOHIM give peoples their tongues (languages). See Genesis 11:1-9. Amen.

39. YAHUSHUA Messiah (JESUS Christ) spoke Hebrew. See Acts 26:14-15. Amen.

40. ELOHIM's Eyes are in "every place", watching everything. See Proverbs 15:3. Amen.

41. It is a known truth (or should be known) that YAHWEH uses the term "man" and "he" to include "everyone" in general including "woman" and "women". Man and woman are

"Mankind" or "Human" alike, that's why both genders has "man" in them. This is referring to a specific "species", not sex, and thus distinguishes between humans and animals, etc. For direct confirmation of this, you can see how ELOHIM addresses woman specifically as man by stating, "he is clean", in Leviticus 13:38-39. Amen. Moreover, it should also be known that we are all (males and females) the "sons" of ELOHIM (GOD), because our true identity is "spirit", and spirits are androgynous (or sexless). It is only when we take on a human "body" that we identify ourselves with whatever sexual organ or part we have. Nevertheless we are not our "physical human bodies" or "earthly bodies", but spiritual bodies (beings) that utilize human bodies to have human experiences, albeit temporarily, and then we discard those temporary bodies and put back on our true self (the spirit), and then move on into the eternal. Apostle Paul spoke of our spiritual/heavenly bodies as being our "glorious" bodies, and putting on our "incorruptible" and "immortal" bodies (spiritual bodies). See 1 Corinthians 15:44,51-53 + Philippians 3:20-21. Amen.

42. YAHUSHUA called Himself the "Son of Adam" (the first Man). Hence, everywhere in your Holy Bible where it calls Him the "Son of Man" was translated from the original "Son of Adam", for the name "Adam" means "Man", anyway. Christ is the Truth, and the truth is that "every" human being born of a woman (for even the first woman name was Adam, until Adam called her name "Eve": "because she was the mother of all living"),is the son of Adam (the first man and first human being). See Genesis 2:21-23; 3:20. YAHUSHUA also came to earth to be a Living Example and show us how to be humble by embracing our hu'man'ness, so much so that He not only identified Himself as a "Man", but a little lower, "the Son of Man", and of course the son is usually less than the father. He showed us the correct way to walk humbly with our EL. See St. John 13:15 + Micah 6:8. That is one of the chief reasons He called Himself the Son of Adam (man) while on Earth. Amen.

43. Be assured, not only does our Great ELOHIM knows the past and the present, He also knows the "future". Amen. In Deuteronomy 31:16-21, EL revealed that He "know their thoughts which they are forming today, even before I bring them to the land of which I swore to give them". And in Verse 16, He tells Moshay, "this people will rise and play the harlot with the gods of the foreigners of the land….See also Isaiah 45:21; 42:9 + Jeremiah 1:5; 29:11. Amen. Even when you think of Adam and Eve's first sin, which caused what many call "the fall of man", ELOHIM the CREATOR already knew that they were going to sin, but He chose to not take away their "freewill". The evidence of this knowledge is in ELOHIM's sacrifice of His Lamb being slain "from the foundation of the world", meaning "before" man was created on the sixth day of creation. See Revelation 13:8b. Amen.

44.ELOHIM speaks about a fire being kindled in His wrath that burns to the "lowest hell" (revealing that there is more than one hell or at least "levels" of hell); similarly, there are more than one Heaven). In the next Verse He says, "I gather evils upon them"- which no doubt refers to "evildoers", because inanimate objects do not have the ability to be evil; people do. These "evildoers" and "wicked ones" (Satan and his angels/followers) will be "turned into hell" and burning in the Lake of Fire and Brimstone forever. See Deuteronomy 32:22-23 + Psalm 9:17 + St. Matthew 25:41 + Revelation 20:10. Amen. It would be wise, however, to compare different Versions of The Holy Bible on these Verses, always including the most authoritative Version in English, the Authorized "King James Version" (KJV). Amen.

45.Moshey died at age 120; his eyes were not dim nor his freshness gone. See Deuteronomy 37:4. Amen.

46.The sun can "see" (has sight). See 2 Samuel 12:11-12. Amen.

47.ELOHIM created all souls. See Isaiah 57:16; and yes, souls can die. See Ezekiel 18:4. Amen.

48.ELOHIM dwells in a high and lofty place, and with those of a contrite and humble spirit and heart. See Isaiah 57:15. Amen.

49.Besides JESUS, there were at least two others that were "perfect" and called such in the Holy Bible: Noah and Job. See Genesis 6:9 (KJV) + Job 1:1 (KJV). Amen.

50.At lease two people are mentioned as "walking with ELOHIM": (1) Enoch. See Genesis 5:22-24; (2) Noah. See Genesis 6:9. Amen. Enoch's walk with EL was so intimate that EL took him away to heaven to be with Him, so that he would not see death. See spec. Verse 24. Amen.

51. The number of days in a year coincide with the number of years Enoch lived on Earth before he was taken away: 365. See Genesis 5:23. Amen.

52. Although vengeance is YHWH's, "one" of the ways He execute vengeance is by using humans to execute vengeance for Him, especially on other humans. See Ezekiel 25:14 + Genesis 9:5-6. Amen. Also, King David, a servant of YHWH, was used by ELOHIM to execute vengeance in the form of warfare upon the enemies of YHWH ELOHIM and the enemies of ADONAI's chosen people Israel. See also Ezekiel 25:14 where YHWH ELOHIM specifically says, "And I will lay My vengeance upon Edom by the hand of My people Israel: and they shall do in Edom according to Mine anger and according to My fury; and they shall know My vengeance, saith YHWH ELOHIM." (KJV). Amen.

53. There are over 600 Laws in the Tanakh (Old Testament) of the Holy Bible. Amen.

54. Ya'aqob strove with ELOHIM and prevailed against His Angel. See Hosea 12:2-5 + Genesis 32:24-28. Amen.

55. The Name of our FATHER in Heaven is "YHWH ELOHIM" of hosts. In English that reads "The LORD GOD" of hosts. "Of hosts" meaning "of all". He is the MOST HIGH over all and everything. Amen. "YHWH" is pronounced "YOD HAY WAW HEY" in Hebrew, and "YAHWEH" in English. "ELOHIM" is pronounced "L-OH-HEEM" in both Hebrew and English. ELOHIM Names are both "Titles" and "Names", similar to how one's name can be "King", and that person is a king also. Many people try to argue that GOD prefers to be called by only His Personal Names, not titles. However, one must remember that GOD is not a "man" that he shall lie! Although we call Him FATHER, and even the Word referenced Him as a "Man of war", that is mostly for the human

finite mind to grasp concepts of Him and who He is, such as Protector, Provider, and the Most Compassionate, but discerningly and truthfully, He is much greater than both a FATHER and a Man, because He is GOD! Even GOD ALMIGHTY. And it's logical that the CREATOR GOD would like to be known and addressed as such, although many acknowledge those as only "Titles". The average man may get offended if you call him "a man" or say "excuse me man", if he know that you know that his personal name is, say for instance, "James"; although he is a man, he may say "you know my name, call me by my name". In comparison, however, a Doctor may get offended if you do not address him or her by their "Title". If, for instance their name and title is "Dr. Marie", and you just address her as "Marie", she may (and most likely will) feel offended due to the lack of respect of not addressing her by her title. And rightfully so, especially with the fact that most doctors go to school and college for many long years and put in much effort and work to earn and be rewarded such an honorable title. Some would even prefer you to call them "Doctor", without the personal name attached, rather than you calling them their personal name without their honorable title attached. For there are so many "Marie's", but not so many "Doctor Marie's". Another example would be a Court Judge, who everyone usually addresses as "Your Honor". That is a Title; nevertheless, the judge prefers or even likes being called that rather than by their name, even if one puts Mrs. or Mr. in the front of their name. Thus, ELOHIM titles are just as important as His Personal names. Nevertheless, it is extremely paramount to know GOD's personal Names also, and He even requires such in Verses that reveal that "all who call upon the 'Name' of the LORD shall be saved". See Romans 10:13 + Acts 2:21. Amen. This Verse places emphasis on the Name of YHWH or His Son YAHUSHUA Messiah (JESUS Christ), because if emphasis wasn't being stressed on the Name here, that Verse would have read "all who call upon the LORD shall be saved".

One of the most important things to remember when considering all of ELOHIM's Personal Sacred Names and Divine Titles is that all of them is referring to the same ELOHIM (GOD/EL/ELOAH). For ELOHIM is not the author of confusion, but of shalom! See 1 Corinthians 14:33. Amen. Therefore do not get to thinking that you are talking about more than one GOD when you address Him by different of His Names and Titles. The different only emphasizes certain of His Characteristics, Personality, and Divinity, such as "EL" or "ELOAH" emphasizes His "Oneness", "ELOHIM" emphasizes Him as 'The CREATOR" and "The MOST HIGH LIVING GOD who created all, everyone, and everything, and thus has ALL and ULTIMATE POWER", "EL SHADDAI" emphasizes Him as "ALMIGHTY" and "ALL POWERFUL", "YHWH" or "YAHWEH" emphasizes Him as "SAVIOR and LORD and RULER over all", "YAHWEH RAPHA" or "JEHOVAH RAPHA", emphasizes Him as "HEALER and CURER of all diseases." And His other names and Titles emphasizes other of His Sacred Attributes and Divine Qualities, but He is the ONE and Same and Only EL/ELOHIM/EL SHADDAI. See Amos 4:13; 5:27 + Genesis 1:1 (in Hebrew). Amen.

56. The word "Anointing" appears more times in the one Verse of 1 John 2:27 (NLT) than in any other Verse in the Holy Bible: 3 times. Amen.

57. Since ELOHIM is the Most Merciful, the Most Compassionate, the Most Gracious, and the Most Patient and Longsuffering, He sometimes relents and changes His Mind concerning the evil and disaster He intends to do to the wicked, especially if they repent. See Jonah 3:10 (MEV) + Psalms 110:4 + Jeremiah 18:7-10 + Ezekiel 18:21-23. Amen.

58.EL is abounding in mercy to those who do not know any better (who does not know right from wrong). See Jonah 4:11 + 1 Timothy 1:13. Amen.

59.ELOHIM creates good and evil, and has the power to send or stop a calamity. See Isaiah 45:7 (KJV) + Micah 1:2-3 (MEV). Amen.

60.ELOHIM Loved Ya'aqob and hated Esau. See Malachi 1:2-3. Amen.

61.We are to bless, magnify, praise, worship, and exalt YAHWEH ELOHIM, the MOST HIGH. See Hosea 11:7 + Isaiah 43:21 + Psalms 99:5. Amen.

62.Whether closely or distantly, "all" human beings are related because of at least two truths: (1) We are all descendants of the same human father and mother (parents), the first Parents of us all (Adam and Eve); (2) ELOHIM made all men and nations from "one blood", thus revealing that all peoples have the same DNA makeup. See Acts 17:26-27. Amen.

63.JESUS did many miracles in Chapter 9 of St. Matthew, including healing a man that was sick of the palsy, healing a woman that had an issue of blood for 12 years, and raising a maid from the dead. Amen.

64.The names of JESUS original or first Disciples/Apostles are: (1) Simon Peter; (2) Andrew; (3) James; (4) John; (5) Philip; (6) Bartholomew; (7) Thomas; (8) Matthew; (9) James (the other); (10) Lebbeus Thaddeus; (11) Simon the Canaanite; (12) Judas Iscariot (who betrayed JESUS, and was replaced by Matthias). See St. Matthew 10:2-4 and Acts 1:23-26. Amen.

65.Wisdom brightens our countenance and causes our face to shine literally. See Ecclesiastes 8:1 + Exodus 34:29-30. Amen.

66.The world will come to an end. See St. Matthew 13:39-40; 28:19-20 + 2 Peter 3. Amen.

67.The HOLY GHOST (HOLY SPIRIT) is GOD (ELOHIM). See 1 John 5:7 (KJV) + Acts 5:3-4. The HOLY SPIRIT is JESUS' FATHER and JESUS' "only" FATHER is ELOHIM (GOD). For the Virgin Mary was with Child from the HOLY SPIRIT. See St. Matthew 1:18-20. See also St. John 4:24 + 1 Peter 1:16: GOD is Holy and He is a Spirit= HOLY SPIRIT. Amen.

68.For JESUS came to save that which was lost; He was manifested to take away our sins. He was and is sinless. See 1 John 3:5 + St. Matthew 18:11. Amen.

69.Hereafter is a brief list of holy men of EL that has been to prison: St. John the Baptist (See St. Matthew 14:3); St. Peter (See Acts 12:5); Apostle Paul (See Acts 16:23); Prophet Jeremiah (See Jeremiah 32:2). Amen.

70.Christ has a specific Law called "The Law of Christ", which is one with "The Law Of LOVE", which teaches us to LOVE the FATHER and each other, and to "bear one another's burdens". JESUS ensured that that is how all men will know that we are His disciples. See Galatians 6:2 + St. Matthew 22:37-40 + St. John 13:35. And perceivably, since JESUS and the FATHER is One, He is what GOD is: LOVE. See 1 John 4:7-21. Amen.

71.Whosoever has seen JESUS Christ has seen the FATHER. In each of the statements by the Messiah found in St. John 12:45; 14:8-11; and 10:30, He unequivocally revealed and confirmed exactly who He is and the Truth of Hid Deity. Amen.

72.ELOHIM LOVEs a cheerful giver. See 2 Corinthians 9:7. Amen.

73.ELOHIM LOVEs them that Loves, considers, and cares for the poor, and He blesses them. See Psalms 41:1-2 + Proverbs 19:17. Amen. We ought to be generous with our giving, for it all comes from the FATHER in heaven, and the more we give the more we receive: and it is actually more blessed to give than to receive. See St. James 1:17 + St. Luke 6:38 + Acts 20:35. Amen.

74.We must enter into the Kingdom of ELOHIM through much "tribulation". See Acts 14:22. Amen. For Satan knows what his final destination is, and he's trying to devour and take as many souls as he can to hell with him. Thus, following the straight and narrow path is not easy, but it is possible. See 1 Peter 5:8 + St. Matthew 7:13-14. Amen.

75.In 1 Corinthians 15:45-47, it speaks about "two Adams"("Man"): the second Adam is the Adon (Lord) from heaven; that's why JESUS called Himself the Son of "Man", which means the Son of "Adam": for in Hebrew "Man" means "Adam", thus, with the knowledge of this Verse, Christ was essentially proclaiming Himself to be the Son of the ADON (LORD) in heaven, or in other words, the Son of Himself, because He is and was and is the ADON (LORD) from and in heaven. See also Psalm 110:1 + St. John 10:10. Amen. The exalted GOD sometimes addresses or talks to/with the humility that is within Himself. But even that humble GOD that is within the exalted GOD is still GOD, because GOD is ONE GOD. Amen.

76.Those who belong to Christ are discerned or recognized by their "lifestyles": for they are distinguished in that they "crucify their flesh with the affections and lusts" thereof. In other words, they are true "Christians": Christ-like in character, moral, speech, and even thoughts. For it suffice that a disciple/follower be like unto his Master/Leader. See Galatians 5:24; 2:20 + 2 Corinthians 5:17 + St. Luke 6:40 + 1 Corinthians 2:16. Amen.

77.YHWH ELOHIM restores the youthfulness of those who faithfully pray to Him and patiently waits upon Him. Amen. See Isaiah 40:30-31 + Job 33:25-26. Amen.

78.The Truth of JESUS' statement, "the first shall be last, and the last first", can be seen in the Passage of 2 Peter 2:5, as where, although Noah was the first of eight to be saved (for he was the "first" one called by ELOHIM, and he prepared the other seven), he was now called the "eight" or "last" person (since it were only eight), in the heretofore mentioned Passage. Amen.

79.Those who hunger and thirst for righteousness shall be filled with the HOLY GHOST(HOLY SPIRIT). See St. Matthew 5:6 + St. John 7:37-39. Amen.

80.YHWH ELOHIM sometimes calls men (and women) by their names, and sometimes "audibly". This is what is meant by one's "calling" from EL SHADDAI. Then after your "calling", He reveals to you your position or positions, and your assignment or assignments, and your office or offices. Similar to how your "boss" can give you more than one position and assignment or even job, GOD chooses to give certain of His men and women of GOD more than one of these stewardships. See Exodus 31:1-4 + 1 Samuel 3:4-10 + St. Matthew 25:14-30 + 1 Peter 4:10. Amen.

81.ADONAI knows our "works", and we receive rewards for our "good works". Moreover, faith without "works" is dead! See 1 Corinthians 3:13-14 + Revelation 2:2a, 13a, 19, 23b, 26-27; 3:1-2, 8, 15; 20:12-13; 21:7. See also St. James 2:17-18. Amen.

82.According to the "Ancient Sacred Calendar" or Jewish Calendar, the first month of the year is "March", and the last month is "February". Sometimes the Jewish year adds up to thirteen months, however, when all of the additional days are grouped together to make another whole month. According to the American

Calendar, "Valentine's Day" is a Jewish "Holyday" which the Jews have been celebrating (albeit according to the ancient sacred calendar) since the days of Esther and Mordecai. See Esther 8:17; 9:19. Amen. Furthermore, Christmas Day or the celebrated Day of the Birth of Christ according to the ASC is February 25, or February 26 if the sun was already set or gone down on the 25th, at the exact time He was Born.

83.One can "become" a Jew, even if not born one. See Esther 8:17. Amen. A real Jew is he or she that is one "inwardly". See Romans 2:29 (and its context). Amen.

84.Hell fire is never quenched. See St. Mark 9:43-47. Amen.

85.Wisdom has children. See St. Matthew 11:19. Amen. JESUS Christ has children that ELOHIM has given Him. See Hebrews 2:13. Amen.

86.ELOHIM is a SPIRIT and His SPIRIT is invisible. See St. John 4:24 + Colossians 1:15. Amen.

87.One of the most ironic statements of YAHWEH in the Holy Bible is in Exodus 34:7, where He proclaims forgiveness of sins and mercy "for thousands", and yet in the same Verse He makes known that He will "by no means clear the guilty; visiting the iniquity of the fathers upon the children...". At first glance, one may assume this statement to be contradictory, especially if you are under the impression that whosoever has sinned is "guilty". Nevertheless, again, one must remember that man does not see how YHWH sees. Man looks at the outer appearance; ELOHIM looks at the "inner": heart, spirit, mind, etc. Therefore the truth of the matter is that ELOHIM is proclaiming mercy and forgiveness unto those who "repent"(Repentance= feeling godly sorrow for one's sins, confessing them and then turning away from them, and then having a changed/renewed mind, walking in newness of behavior, now living a righteous life), but His wrath is upon those who refuse to repent: those are the guilty ones, the ones who reject His mercy and salvation. See Ezekiel 18:21-23 + 2 Chronicles 7:14 + 1 John 1:9 + Proverbs 28:13 + 2 Corinthians 7:10 + 1 Samuel 16:7 + Revelation 2:21 + Romans 12:2. Amen.

88.Good parenting "requires" that you discipline your child, even "beating" them when necessary. For all children do inappropriate things at times, requiring correction, teaching, and sometimes chastening. For even IMMANU'EL (JESUS) had to "learn to reject the evil and choose the good", and He was GOD ALMIGHTY in the flesh! (See Isaiah 7:14) Amen. Thus, how much so "all" children have to "learn" the same. The sternness of the discipline depends on the severity of the offense. Not every offense requires a beating with the "rod", and neither does every offense demands only a simple "that's wrong. Don't do it again." For the Word of YHWH admonishes us that if we Love our children, we ought to beat them (and there is no man nor woman on the planet Earth that's a better Parent and Teacher than ELOHIM). Of course the beating should not be in a child abuse manner, but a good beating can change their behavior and save their souls from hell. See Proverbs 23:13-14; 22:6. Amen.

89.The lesson learned from 1 Timothy 6:6-8 and 1 John 2:17 is "be content with what you have, with what EL bless you with. Never be greedy, give to the needy; and never cherish what perish." See also Proverbs 30:7-9; 31:30. Amen.

90.The LORD YHWH is the One who opens wombs, enabling women to conceive and bear children. See Genesis 29:31; 30:2 + Psalms 127:3. Amen.

91.All saints are family and shall treat each other as such. See Galatians 3:26 + 1 Timothy 5:1-2 + Psalm 82:6 + 1 Peter 3:8. Amen.

92.Leah, the mother of some of Jacob's (Israel's) children, including Judah, was a kind of "Seer"; for she perceived (saw) what YAHWEH saw, and what He showed and revealed to her. Compare Genesis 29:31 with 29:32-35. Amen.

93.The elders who labor in preaching and teaching are worthy of double honor. See 1 Timothy 5:17. Amen.

94.Getting or being "drunk" with wine (alcohol) is a sin called "dissipation" and "debauchery" See Ephesians 5:18 (NKJV). And "drunkards" shall not enter into the kingdom of heaven. See 1 Corinthians 6:9-10 + Galatians 5:19-21. Amen.

95.Not "money" per se, but the "love of money" is the root of all evil. See 1 Timothy 6:9-10. Amen. In this context, "the love of money" does not only means the tangible gold or silver or paper or coins, but also includes any and all kinds of illegal, unjust, or dishonest "gain", such as being greedy, whether it's for power or prestige or even a for a position that is not rightfully yours. For example, GOD is GOD because He is GOD and always has been GOD and always will be GOD, not because someone "made" Him GOD. Thus, when Lucifer attempted to become GOD or higher than GOD, he fell into this context of "loving money" (unrightful power/position), seeking something that did not belong to him and never would. And since this sin is the first sin ever, it is the "root" of all sin: the beginning or starting point. See Ezekiel 28:12-19 + Revelation 12:9. Amen.

96.Christ JESUS is "everyone's" Chief Example of how to live a "perfect life" pleasing to the FATHER. See St. John 13:13-15 + 1 Peter 2:21-25 + St. Matthew 5:48. Amen.

97.JESUS Christ is the King of kings and the Lord of lords (Sovereign). See 1 Timothy 6:15 + Revelation 19:16. Amen.

98.ADONAI (The LORD) will return. See St. James 5:8 + Philippians 4:5 + 1 Timothy 6:14 + Revelation 22:20 + 1 Thessalonians 4:13-17 + 2 Peter 3:10-12. Amen.

99.YAHUSHUA Messiah dwells in unapproachable Light, which no man has seen or can see. See 1 Timothy 6:16 + 1 John 1:5 + St. John 8:12; 12:46. Amen.

100.Teachings for the man or woman of ELOHIM. See 1 Timothy 6:11-12. Amen.

101.One can be baptized "for" the dead, but not "in the name" of the dead. See 1 Corinthians 15:29. Amen. JESUS Christ (YESHUA, IMMANUEL YAHUSHUA Messiah) is the only Name anyone and everyone should be baptized in: "…in the Name of the FATHER, and of the Son, and of the HOLY GHOST (HOLY SPIRIT)." See St. Matthew 28:19 + Acts 2:38. Amen.

102.ELOHIM created creation "good". See Genesis 1. Amen. YHWH ELOHIM created every creature "good". It is the creatures themselves, however, which goes out and corrupt themselves, thus becoming "bad". See 1 Timothy 4:4-5. Amen. Even Lucifer was created good and beautiful, and was "perfect" in his ways from the day he was created, till iniquity was found in him. See Ezekiel 28:11-19. Amen.

103.The Word, even ADONAI Christ the Messiah's Word, will Judge every man and woman that rejects Christ and His words. See St. John 12:48. Amen.

104.Although we are not under the Law, but under grace, we must still obey the Law. See Romans 6:14. For even Christ Himself obeyed ELOHIM's Law, and announced that He did not come to abolish or destroy the Law, but to fulfill it. See St. Matthew 5:17-19. Amen. Although ELOHIM does not require the doing of certain ancient Laws, such as sacrificing sheep and goats, etc., for atonement of sins, many of His Laws that He gave us are "perpetual", meaning that they are meant to be kept and obeyed "forever", for as long as the Earth remains. Amen. Hereafter is a nice, but not exhaustive, list of such perpetual Laws: The Ten Commandments, written with the Finger of ELOHIM. See Exodus 20:1-17 + Deuteronomy 5:6-22 + Exodus 31:18; Sabbath keeping, Exodus 31:15-17; prohibition on eating fat or blood, Leviticus 3:17 + 17:10-16; observing the Passover, and the Feast of Unleavened Bread, and the Feast of Tabernacles, Exodus 12:17-24; the continuous burning of the Lamp, Exodus 27:20-21; The Law Of Christ, Galatians 6:2; the Law of Sowing and Reaping, Galatians 6:7-8; the Law of Justice, Isaiah 3:10-11; and The Law of LOVE(GOD), which fulfills the whole Law: See St. Matthew 22:36-40 + Romans 13:10 + Galatians 5:14. Amen.

105.ELOHIM is very merciful. See Exodus 32:11-14 + St. James 5:11. Amen.

106.EL offers Eternal Life to all believers. See St. John 3:16 + 1 John 5:11-13 + Romans 6:23. Amen.

107.What EL requires of us: See Deuteronomy 10:12-13 "And now, Israel, what does the LORD your GOD require of you, but to fear the LORD your GOD, to walk in all His ways and to Love Him, to serve YHWH your ELOHIM with all your heart and with all your soul, and to keep the Commandments of YHWH and His Statutes which I command you today for your good?" Amen. See also Micah 6:8, "He has shown you, O man, what is good; and what does the LORD require of you but to do justly, to Love mercy, and to walk humbly with your EL?" Amen.

108.We reap what we sow. See Galatians 6:7-8 + Isaiah 3:10-11. Amen. Many people like to call this "Karma", or "what goes around comes around". The real name is the Law of Sowing and

Reaping; and it works for both, the good and the bad. If you sow a good seed of goodness or righteousness to someone by doing them right or good, good will come back to you and on you. If on the other hand, however, you sow a bad seed of wrongfulness by doing someone wrong or harming them unjustly, then wrong, hurt, and injustice will come back to you and on you. Amen.

109. We are saved by Hope. See Romans 8:24 (Authorized King James Version); and we are saved by Grace through Faith. See Ephesians 2:8-9; and we are saved by calling upon the "Name" of YHWH. See Romans 10:13. Amen.

110. Godliness (Spiritual Discipline + Virtue) is much more valuable than physical training and exercise, because it has "eternal" value as opposed to the temporary satisfaction that the physical offers. This is not to say we are to abandon our physical bodies, well-being, and health, but rather that we put the greater emphasis, effort, time, and training on our spirit and spiritual health, which is absolutely more important since that is the part of us that will remain forever, our essence, even after our physical bodies perish. See 1 Timothy 4:8: 6:6. Amen.

111. Similar to storms and hurricanes of our day, storms were named even back in Apostle Paul's day. See Acts 27:14. Amen.

112. There are "two" resurrections. See Revelation 20:5. Amen.

113. Those who hear, keep, and "do" the Word of ELOHIM are moreso blessed, or at least equally blessed as the Blessed Virgin Mary (the Mother of Christ, the Son of GOD). See St. Luke 11:27-28 + St. Matthew 12:46-50 + St. James 1:22. Amen.

114. Abraham is the father of "all" believers (the faithful), whether circumcised or uncircumcised. See Romans 4:11-12 + Galatians 3:7. Amen.

115.GOD Name as "JAH", "YAH", and "JEHOVAH" appears even in English Holy Bibles. See Psalms 68:4; 83:18 (KJV) + Exodus 6:3 + Isaiah 12:2; 26:4. Amen. YHWH ELOHIM, the CREATOR and ALMIGHTY MOST HIGH GOD, appears to people by different Names, but He is still the same One and Only Living GOD the FATHER. See Exodus 6:3. Amen.

116.JESUS Christ shall never die again, He shall never "taste" death again. See Romans 6:9-10 + 1 Peter 3:18. Amen.

117,Moses, the man of ELOHIM, instructed the Israelites to "circumcise the foreskin of your heart…". See Deuteronomy 10:16 (Compare Romans 2:29). Amen.

118.Satan bounds people with infirmities, deformities, diseases, sicknesses, etc. See St. Luke 13:16. Amen.

119.JESUS Christ saves, heals, delivers, and rescues. See Acts 10:38 + St. Luke 13:10-17. Amen.

120.We are all created by ELOHIM, but all are not the children of ELOHIM. ELOHIM gives us free will of choice to choose whether to be His child, or a child of the devil. We choose by who we Love and obey. For Satan has children; they are the wicked evildoers. See St. John 8:44 + 1 John 3:8,10 + 2 Timothy 2:26. Amen. ELOHIM's children are those who are holy and live righteous lives. See 1 John 3:10. Amen. Moreover, we are made the children of ELOHIM through our faith in His only "begotten Son" YESHUA Messiah and our acceptance of Him. See St. John 1:12-13 + Galatians 3:26. Amen.

121.Only those who are "of faith" (have faith) are children of Abraham, the Friend of ELOHIM; for ELOHIM has designated Abraham the father of the faithful (those who have faith). See Galatians 3, specifically Verse 7. Amen.

122.The Word "Love" or "Loved" appears nine times in 1 Corinthians (the LOVE Chapter), and twenty-seven times in the fourth Chapter of 1st John. The Holy Bible itself is YHWH ELOHIM's LOVE Letter to us, His children. Amen.

123.YAHUSHUA not only Commands us to "be perfect", He also "requires" it. See St. Matthew 5:48 + Revelation 3:2. Amen.

124.Our father Abraham (the father of all who have faith) is also a "Prince", as he was called in Genesis 23:6 (KJV). Amen.

125.After we repent, whether it is before or after we come to Christ, it is time to do "works", specifically "good works", which is the will of ELOHIM, and the reason for Him giving us His Word (the Holy Scriptures). The Word of EL teaches us what to "do" and how to live. See 2 Timothy3:16-17 + Revelation 2:5 + St. James 2:14-26; 1:22. Amen.

126.Wisdom is the "principal thing". See Proverbs 4:7. Amen.

127.The Way of Wisdom. See Proverbs 4:11 (compare St. John 14:6: Wisdom and JESUS Christ are One) + St. Luke 7:35 + St. Matthew 11:19. Amen.

128.Christ received glory from the FATHER ELOHIM, and King Solomon received glory from Christ (or at least the recognition of it). See St. Matthew 6:29. Amen.

129.We are the "circumcision" who worship ELOHIM in the Spirit and rejoice in JESUS Christ. See Philippians 3:3. Amen.

130.In every instance where man or woman is called "dog" in the Holy Bible, it is in a derogatory and degrading sense. See Philippians 3:2 + St. Matthew 15:26; 7:6 + Revelation 22:15. The latter revealing that "dogs", and the like, will be outside of the gate of Heaven; meaning dogs will not enter into the Kingdom of Heaven. Amen.

131.Christ came to save sinners by calling them to repentance and placing their trust in Him as their personal Lord and Savior, obeying Him and doing the FATHER's will. See 1 Timothy 1:15 + St. Luke 5:32 + St. Mark 2:17 + St. Matthew 7:21. Amen.

132.The three scariest Verses for sinners (and really in general) in the Holy Bible are: (1) Revelation 20:13-15; (2) Hebrews 10:26-27; (3) Hebrews 10:31. Amen.

133.For the godly who have experienced the lost of their property or destruction of their possessions, there is true hope and comfort found in Hebrews 10:34 + St. Matthew 6:20. Amen.

134.It is not a sin, in itself, to drink wine, unless you are under a vow to not drink. Drinking wine becomes a sin whenever one over-indulge in it or drink in excess, thus becoming "drunk". Moreover, it is even recommended in Scripture that one should drink wine for certain infirmities, and for one's "stomach's sake". See 1 Timothy 5:23 + 1 Peter 4:3. Amen. And JESUS turned water into wine, and of course He didn't do it so that they people can sin, but that they may enjoy themselves, have a nice time (at the wedding) with a merry heart. See St. John 2:1-11 + Psalm 104:15 + Ecclesiastes 10:19. However, anyone who is in a position of authority (such as princes, kings, and judges) would be wise to abstain from any and all forms of drinking wine or strong drink, as even a little can alter your state of mind and distort reality, thus causing you to make unsound, unjust, or downright foolish judgments. See Proverbs 20:1. Amen.

135.ELOHIM (GOD the FATHER) has given Christ children. Wherefore it is true that JESUS Christ has children. See Hebrews 2:13. Amen.

136.The name "Melchizedek" means "Righteous King" and "King of Salem(Peace)", and he is a Priest of the MOST HIGH

ELOHIM. See Hebrews 7:1-3. Amen. He is the only other being besides ELOHIM and ELOHIM's Son JESUS Christ that has "no beginning of days". Moreover, he has no father nor mother but is made like unto "the Son of ELOHIM (GOD)". See Hebrews 7:3-4. Amen.

137.If anyone slay a witch solely on the fact that she is a witch, the slayer is justified and shall not be punished on the basis and authority of the Scriptures. See specifically Exodus 22:18. Amen. A witch shall not be allowed to live. Amen.

138.Whosoever performs a sexual act with a beast or any animal shall be put to death. See Exodus 22:19. Amen.

139.Whosoever sacrifices to any god except the LORD GOD (YHWH ELOHIM) shall be utterly destroyed. See Exodus 22:20. Amen.

140.ELOHIM do not play about widows and the fatherless (meaning He is extra strict about them). See Exodus 22:22-24 + Psalms 68:5. Amen. For He has a special care and concern for them. Amen.

141.EL SHADDAI is the King of the saints. See Revelation 15:3. Amen.

142.A Hebrew slave shall not serve for more than six years, unless he agrees to it. See Exodus 21:2-6. Amen.

143.Whoeoever, with guile, intentionally slays a man shall be put to death. See Exodus 21:14. Amen.

144.Whosoever killeth their father or mother shall be put to death. See Exodus 21:15. Amen.

145.Whosoever curses their father or mother shall be put to death. See Exodus 21:17. Amen.

146.Whosoever kidnaps or abducts someone shall be put to death. See Exodus 21:16. Amen.

147.ELOHIM often speaks of man and woman interchangeably: for His Words and Messages to "men" usually always includes "women", and "he" and "him" usually includes "she" and "her", unless otherwise noted as being specifically for men only or to men only. See Exodus 21:20-21 (KJV). Amen.

148.It is "blood" that purifies things. The Blood of Christ specifically cleanses the penitent sinner from his sins, thus purifying him, making him "born again" and a "new creature in Christ". See Hebrews 9:22 + 2 Corinthians 5:17. Amen.

149.Although ELOHIM is the Most Merciful, He is also the Most Just, and there comes a point when the accumulation of sin becomes unbearable to Him, and no sacrifice for sins will be permitted. This point comes mainly on two occasions: (1) On Judgment Day, of course, there will be no more time to "get right" with the LORD, or put one's "house in order"; if one hasn't already done these things, they will be condemned on Judgment Day. And (2) Whenever someone acquires the knowledge of the truth and rejects it and proceeds to sin willfully, EL then metes out discipline, punishment, and or condemnation to the willful sinner. See Hebrews 10:26-31. Amen.

150.ELOHIM gave Christ JESUS the "full" measure of His Spirit. See St. John 3:34 + Colossians 1:19 (KJV). Amen.

151.We fulfill "The Law of Christ" when we bear one another's burdens. See Galatians 6:2. Amen.

152.We can and ought to bless YHWH ELOHIM. Some folks believe and proclaim that the LORD GOD can bless us, but we cannot bless Him; however, this is not biblically sound. The truth is we can and ought to bless GOD the FATHER. See St. Luke 24:52-53 + 1 Peter 1:3 + Psalms 103:1-5; 104:1-5 (KJV). Amen.

153. The month of "Abib" (March) is really the first month of the year, according to the Ancient Sacred Calendar (ASC), that is the Hebrew/Jewish Calendar; this is the month that YHWH ELOHIM brought the children of Israel up out of the land of Egypt (bondage/slavery). It should be noted that some years the ASC possesses thirteen months, whenever the extra days of the year add up to an additional month. See Exodus 12:1,11; 13:4. Amen.

154. The HOLY GHOST is the SPIRIT of ELOHIM= The HOLY SPIRIT. See Acts 16:6-7 + 1 John 5:7 (KJV). Amen.

155. Wisdom is a "Tree of Life". See Proverbs 3:18. Amen.

156. YAHWEH has a "secret counsel", which He confides and shares with His chosen ones. See Proverbs 3:32 + Amos 3:7 (His servants the prophets). Amen.

157. ELOHIM is the Most Gracious. See Exodus 22:27. Amen.

158. ELOHIM is the MOST HIGH GOD, and His children are little "gods". See Psalms 82:6 + Exodus 22:28. Amen.

159. One must have the Spirit of EL to know the things of EL. See 1 Corinthians 2:11-12. Amen.

160. YHWH's Word is "forever" settled in heaven. See Psalms 119:89. Amen.

161. Those who reject JESUS will be judged by JESUS' Word on Judgment Day. See St. John 12:48. Amen. For more on the Word, its Power, and Authority, see also St. John 1:1-3 + 1 John 5:7. Amen.

162. There are three classes of people on earth: the Jews, the Gentiles, and the Church of ELOHIM; the Church being One, the Body and Bride of Christ, which consist of both: the believing Jews

and the believing Gentiles. See 1 Corinthians 10:32 + Galatians 3:28. Amen.

163.For the difference between "seasons" and "times", see Genesis 1:14 + Acts 3:19,21; 17:30 + St. Luke 21:24 + Ephesians 1:10 + Ecclesiastes 3:1-8. Amen.

164.The Gentiles have a "will". See 1 Peter 4:3. Amen.

165.The devil has a "will". See 2 Timothy 2:26. Amen.

166.The Ten Commandments are given twice by YHWH ELOHIM in His Word (The Holy Scriptures). See Exodus 20:1-17 + Deuteronomy 5:6-21. Amen.

167.YHWH ELOHIM does not look on the outer appearance of man (as men do), but He looks at a man's heart. See 1 Samuel 16:7 + Acts 13:22. Amen.

168. Though Jacob and Israel is the same person, ELOAH sometimes distinguishes His address to him. See Deuteronomy 33:10 + Numbers 23:23. Amen. The reasons for this is because (1) Jacob is an individual, while Israel is a multitude (all of Jacob's seed that came from his body); (2) Israel is the spiritual name of Jacob, the name that YHWH ELOHIM Himself gave him, as opposed to the name that his parents gave him. See Genesis 32:24-28. Amen.

169. The NKJV (New King James Version) omitted "as a prince" in Genesis 32:28 (compare King James Version [KJV] with New King James Version [NKJV]). The inclusion of this title is significant because it reveals in what capacity Jacob (Israel) gained his victory. See Genesis 32:28. Amen. The name "Israel" literally means "Prince with ELOHIM" (Prince with GOD). Amen.

170.Although we are to do "good works", see 2 Timothy 3:16-17, we are not to "trust in our works" as the source of our righteousness, but our "faith" in Adonai JESUS Christ, and then our good works are the fruit and revelation of our faith in Christ. For no one can honestly say that they Love and trust in JESUS without obeying Him. For Christ said, "You will know who Love Me by their obedience to Me". Works are good and we're supposed to do them-matter of truth, we "have" to do them-in order to enter into the kingdom of heaven; for "doing" the will of the FATHER in heaven means "doing works", not doing nothing. See St. Matthew 7:21. Amen. However, it is error to believe that it is our works that "saves" us. For if this was so, then those people did "good works" in the Name of JESUS would have automatically qualified for entrance into heaven. Nevertheless, the Lord still rejected them. See St. Matthew 7:22-23. The truth is that it is the Lord Himself who saves us when we receive and accept Him, placing our faith and trust in Him and His Blood that was shed for us on calvary, and Him dying and rising again for our forgiveness and redemption . Then we show our appreciation to Him by obeying Him and doing "good works" (the FATHER's will). Therefore, whosoever does not do "good works" (the FATHER's will) is damned already because they have shown that they care less about all that the Messiah did for them, the pain He went through, etc. They are living to do their "own" will, which will not get them into heaven. Even when folks think that are doing what's right and "good works", if it is not what ELOHIM has called you to do, you are still not doing "His" will, but your own. The three main ways to know the FATHER's will for you and your life are: (1) Praying and asking Him what is His will for you and your life; (2) Listening for a response from Him regarding your prayer request to know His will; (3) Reading and studying His Word (the Holy Bible) with the HOLY GHOST helping, assisting, teaching, and guiding you. For all devout Christians and saints know that "faith without works is dead"! See Jeremiah 48:7 + Ephesians 2:8-9 + St. James 2:17 + compare Revelation 3:15-16; 22:12. Amen.

171.Christ cannot die again, according to Scripture. See Romans 6:9-10. Amen.

172.YAHWEH destroyed seven nations to clear the way for the Hebrew Israelites. See Acts 13:19. Amen.

173.For YHWH ELOHIM knows even our minds and thoughts (every one of them!). See Ezekiel 11:5. Amen.

174.Those who say they believe in the Holy Scriptures as the Word of ELOHIM (GOD) call Him a liar if they do not believe that ELOHIM raised JESUS Christ, His Son, from the dead. See 1 John 5:10 + Acts 13:30. Amen.

175.There are two different types of wisdom: wisdom that is from below: worldly/devilish; and the Wisdom that is from above: Heavenly/Godly. See St. James 3:14-17; 1:5. Amen.

176.Our greatest victory and triumph (the way we overcome the evil one and defeat all evil), comes from our faith in Christ, the Blood of the Lamb (JESUS), and the word of our testimony. It is the FATHER who gives us this victory through His Son. See Revelation 12:11 + 1 John 5:4-5 + 1 Corinthians 15:57. Amen.

177.The whole Law of EL is fulfilled in "LOVE": when we LOVE ELOHIM with all our heart, mind, strength, and soul, and Love others as ourselves. This is "The Law of LOVE", which is called "The Royal Law" in St. James 2:8. See Galatians 5:14 + Romans 13:8-10. Amen.

178."The Golden Rule", or Law, is that we are to do unto others as we would have them do unto us. See St. Matthew 7:12. Amen.

179.We are saved by the grace of EL, through faith in Him and His Son JESUS Christ. See Acts 15:11 + Romans 10:9. Amen. Also, we are saved by "hope", which is our confidence of endurance and perseverance. See Romans 8:24. Amen.

180.LOVE covers "all" sins. See Proverbs 10:12 + 1 Peter 4:8. Amen.

181.A man does not necessarily have to be another man's "direct" or "immediate" father to be their father; an older family member (even an uncle or other "ancestor") of the younger man could be considered their father. This truth is witnessed in at least three circumstances in the Holy Bible: (1) Even though many of the "children of Israel" had different biological fathers (such as Reuben and Judah), they are all usually called and known as "the children of Israel (Jacob)"; (2) Although the Gentiles were not born of the Jews or of "the circumcision", yet those who have faith in GOD and Christ are the "children of Abraham" (a Jew); (3) YAHUSHUA Messiah (JESUS Christ) did not even have an "earthly" or "human" father, yet He was called the "son of David", because He descended from the same Kingly Royal Bloodline (Judah) as King David (who was His "ancestor" according to the flesh). See St. Matthew 1:1; 9:27 + Galatians 3:7. Amen.

182.The dream that Jacob had was prophetic in nature, the "Ladder" prophesied JESUS Christ (The Way to Heaven), and the angels ascending and descending upon Him, as Christ revealed. See St. John 1:51. Amen. Compare Genesis 28:12 with St. John 14:6 and 1:51. Amen.

183.The LORD (YHWH) called the Seventh Day the "Sabbath Day", and commanded that we remember it, keep it holy, rest, and do no work on that Day. Also, we are to remain inside our home or Church on that Day and not go out. See Exodus 16:23,29-30; 20:8-11 + Deuteronomy 5:12-15. Amen.

184.YESHUA Christ (JESUS/YAHUSHUA/IMMANUEL Messiah) is the King of kings and the Lord of lords. See 1 Timothy 16:14-16 + Revelation 17:14; 19:16. Amen.

185.We are commanded to rebuke "before all" those who sin, so that others will perceive that sinning is wrong and thus be afraid to sin. For when one is aware that their sin will be exposed, they will be less likely to sin. However, this approach calls for discernment on behalf of the one doing the rebuking, and one must remember that there is a time to rebuke publicly and there is a time to rebuke privately, and there is a time to refrain from rebuking all together. It takes wisdom to know the difference between "meddling" (which involves jumping into other peoples' business without their consent); and correcting/rebuking someone who is clearly wrong. The Key here is to be led by the Spirit of EL SHADDAI and listen to His Voice as to when you are to get involved and say something, and when not to. See Proverbs 26:4-5 + 1 Timothy 5:20 + 1 Peter 4:15 + St. James 4:11-12 + St. Matthew 7:1. Amen. Hence, whatever approach you take, you should do it without making a final judgment or condemnation. You ought to do it to help/correct and enlighten the person so that they can make the proper adjustment and thus avoid being condemned on the Day of Judgment. Amen.

186.A laborer is worthy of their wages. See 1 Timothy 5:18 + St. James 5:4 + St. Luke 10:7. Amen.

187.We are to strive against sin even to the point of having our blood shed. See Hebrews 12:4. Amen.

188.Some demons can only be cast out by "prayer and fasting". See St. Matthew 17:21. Amen.

189.ELOHIM is the CREATOR of all, see Genesis 1; "the FATHER of spirits", see Hebrews 12:9; the OWNER of "all souls", see Ezekiel 18:4; and "the GOD of all flesh", see Jeremiah 32:27. Amen.

190.One can "see" ELOHIM under the right circumstances. See St. Matthew 5:8 + Hebrews 12:14 + Exodus 24:10-11 + 3 John 11 + 1 John 3:6. Amen.

191.The first thing ELOHIM created when He began creating the heavens and the earth was "Light". See Genesis 1:1-5. Compare St. John 1:1-10 and Colossians 1:15 and Romans 8:29. Amen. Please note that while JESUS Christ is called "the firstborn" and the "begotten of the FATHER", He always existed with GOD the FATHER, He has no beginning (His Spirit); only His "physical body" has a beginning. His Spirit is Eternal, and He has the power to grant Eternal Life to all whom He choose. See 1 John 5:11-13. Amen.

192.The whole Chapter 17 of St. John is JESUS' prayer to the FATHER, especially for His disciples and all Christians who believed in Him and His Message (the Gospel) in His time and those who would later hear and believe also. See St. John Chapter 7. Amen.

193.In the King James Version, "Joshua's" name is spelled "Hoshe'a" in Deuteronomy 32:44 (compare KJV with NKJV); and it is known that "Hoshe'a" is really "Joshua", because it mentions "the son of Nun", and Joshua is known to be the son of Nun. Joshua succeeded Moses and became the leader of Israel after Moses' death. See Deuteronomy 34:8- Joshua 1:2. Amen.

194.We will all stand before the Judgment Seat of Christ (to be judged). See Romans 14:10-12 + 2 Corinthians 5:10 + St. John 5:22. Amen.

195.ELOHIM the FATHER, Christ the Son, and the HOLY SPIRIT (the Three that are ONE), all taught and commanded, through Moses (and JESUS Himself) that we (humans/men/women/earthlings) are to "be perfect". See Genesis 17:1 + St. Matthew 5:48 + Deuteronomy 18:13 (KJV). Amen.

196. There is a "MOST HIGH GOD" (YHWH ELOHIM/ YAHWEH EL SHADDAI), and there are lesser "gods" whom He rule over and judge. This MOST HIGH ELOHIM is the only ONE worthy and deserving of "worship"; for He alone is the CREATOR of all. Amen. See Psalms 82; 95:3 + Exodus 12:12. Amen.

197. YAHUSHUA Christ is called "the Just One" in Acts 7:52, and "that Just One" in Acts 22:14. For He is Just, and One with The Most Just (GOD). Amen.

198. YHWH ELOHIM is the CREATOR, MAKER, and OWNER of all souls, spirits, and flesh. See Jeremiah 32:27 + Hebrews 12:9 + Ezekiel 18:4. Amen.

199. The Tribe of Judah ("Yahudah"- the Tribe that JESUS comes from) are called and chosen by YAHWEH ELOHIM to be "Leaders and Lawgivers". See Numbers 2:9 + Psalms 60:7; 108:8. Amen.

200. For "many are called, but few are chosen". Therefore, be sure to make your calling and election sure. See St. Matthew 22:14 + 2 Peter 1:10 + 2 Thessalonians 2:13-14 + Jeremiah 1:5 + Romans 8:29-30. Amen.

201. He that believeth on the Son of ELOHIM has Eternal Life. See St. John 3:16 + 1 John 5:11-13,20. Amen.

202. The FATHER, YHWH ELOHIM, has equipped the Son, YAHUSHUA Christ the Messiah, with "all" power, authority, and dominion; all things belong to Christ! Amen. See St. John 3:34-35 + St. Matthew 28:18. Amen.

Chapter 3:
Great Secrets, Mysteries, and Revelations of The Holy Bible.

(See 1 Corinthians 2:6-7 + 1 Timothy 3:16 + Colossians 1:25-26)

1.The 12 precious stones representing the 12 Tribes of Israel according to Exodus 28:17-21 are as follows: (1) Reuben: Ruby; (2) Simeon: Topaz; (3) Levi: Emerald; (4) Yahudah (Judah): Turquoise; (5) Dan: Sapphire; (6) Naphtali: Diamond; (7) Gad: Jacinth; (8) Asher: Agate; (9) Yissaskar: Amethyst; (10) Zebulun: Beryl; (11) Yoseph (Joseph): Onyx; (12) Benyamin (Benjamin): Jasper. Amen.

2.The kingdom of heaven is not a matter of eating and drinking, see Romans 14:17-18; Nevertheless, we will eat and drink in heaven, see Revelation 7:17. Christ revealed that, after the resurrection, we will not be able to die anymore, but will be equal to the angels, and are "sons of ELOHIM", see St. Luke 20:36. And angels do eat; for the very manna itself that YAHWEH rained down from heaven was "angels' food", see Psalms 78:24-25. Additionally, YAHUSHUA Himself said, "But I say unto you, I will not drink of this fruit of the vine from now on until that day when I drink it anew with you in My FATHER's Kingdom." See St. Matthew 26:29. Amen.

3.You must be counted "worthy" to attain the "age" after the resurrection. See St. Luke 20:35. Amen.

4.The kingdom of ELOHIM (GOD) is "within" you. See St. Luke 17:21. Amen.

5.Contrary to popular belief, prompted even by "scientist", the moon does have its own light. See Isaiah 13:10. Amen.

6.There is a sure way that any and every believer can cast out even the most resistant devil(s), demon(s), or unclean spirit(s). This way is by "prayer and fasting". Amen. See St. Matthew 17:18-21. Amen.

7.Faith is not only a necessity, but it is a "requirement" to have faith. For, first of all, one cannot even please ELOHIM without faith; it is "impossible", see Hebrews 11:6. Amen. And second of all, "anything" said or done without faith is sin. In other words, whatsoever does not proceed from faith is sin. See Romans 14:23. Amen.

8.The Earth is a woman: EL calls the earth "her". See Isaiah 13:13. Amen.

9.YAHWEH ELOHIM rebukes even kings and rulers for His Anointed Ones and Prophets. See Psalms 105:15 + Genesis 20:6-7. Amen.

10.Humans can "make" themselves a new heart and a new spirit, see Ezekiel 18:21. This re-making reveals that we are indeed "gods" as our FATHER ELOHIM (The MOST HIGH GOD) calls us in Psalms 82:6. Amen.

11.Rebellion (disobedience, insubordination) is as the sin of "witchcraft" (sorcery, magic)- which is one of the worst sins to EL SHADDAI; and stubbornness (hardheadedness, being stiff-necked) is as the sin of iniquity (the plotting and planning to commit sin and the forming of intentions and motives to do wrong) and idolatry (worshipping of idols/false gods)- which "is" the worst sin to ELOHIM the CREATOR. For YHWH ELOHIM alone is the CREATOR of all, therefore He alone is deserving and worthy of worship. Amen. Our ELOHIM is rightfully a "Jealous" EL. Amen. See 1 Samuel 15:23 + Exodus 34:14. Amen.

12.Similar to the Noah Flood, the next destroying/devouring of the earth will be by fire. For "…the flaming flame shall not be quenched, and all faces from the South to the North shall be burned therein", is a prophecy found in Ezekiel 20:47-48. Amen. Also, " whereby the world that then was, being overflowed with water, perished: but the heavens and the earth, which are now, by the same Word are kept in store, reserved unto fire against the Day of Judgment and perdition of ungodly men.…But the Day of the LORD will come as a thief in the night…the earth also and the works that are therein shall be burned up". See 2 Peter Chapter 3, specifically Verses 6,7,10 (KJV). Amen.

13.YHWH does not see as man sees; for men look at the outer appearance, but ELOHIM looks at the heart. See 1 Samuel 16:7. Amen.

14.In 1 John 1:1-3, we are exhorted to "test the spirits" to see whether they are of EL. We do this by examining the "fruit" that the "tree" (person) is bearing. The "fruit" being their actions, words, and deeds (reapings). To know whether a spirit is "of ELOHIM", that spirit (through whatever body it possesses) must confess that Christ came in the flesh. However, to know whether a person has the "HOLY SPIRIT" (which is ELOHIM's Highest Spirit, even He Himself, His very presence), that person must live like JESUS lived: blameless. This includes no profane talk (cussing, etc.), no lying, no stealing, no cheating, no sexual immorality, no covetousness, no deceit, and not harming anyone in any way, but rather Loving others as JESUS did. Amen. It should be noted, however, that, at the beginning stages of when the HOLY SPIRIT possesses someone, the person being possessed may still sin sometimes, and that is because he or she is still trying to do their own will and has not yet wholly surrendered to the HOLY SPIRIT and His leading. For it is the Spirit of ELOHIM (the HOLY SPIRIT that makes us "perfect" when we submit completely to Him and His will. Amen.

15. Whereever there is arguing and confusion, ELOHIM is not in its midst. For ELOHIM is not the author of confusion, but of shalom (peace). See 1 Corinthians 14:33 + 2 Timothy 2:16. Amen.

16. The earth can "fear". See Psalms 76:8. Amen.

17. Although vengeance is YHWH's, He sometimes uses humans to execute His vengeance. See Ezekiel 25:14 + 2 Samuel 7:14 + Genesis 9:6. Amen.

18. The two most loyal and obedient kings of ELOHIM, besides King David and King JESUS, were King Hezekiah and King Josiah. See 2 Kings 18:3-7; 23:25. Amen.

19. Besides JESUS Christ, King Solomon was the wisest king- and man in general- to ever walk the face of the earth. He had 700 wives and 300 concubines= 1,000 women lovers. See 1 Kings 3:3-14. And although I noted the many lovers he had, they are not what made him wise; but rather, they led to his downfall. See 1 Kings 11:4. Solomon Loved the LORD YHWH, and his wisdom began when he asked ELOHIM for it (Wisdom) in a prayer that pleased ELOHIM so much that He not only granted Solomon the wisdom, understanding, and knowledge to lead YAHWEH's people and judge them righteously and justly, but He also gave Solomon what Solomon did not request in his prayer (riches and honor), so much so that King Solomon was also the richest and wealthiest man of his generation. See 1 Kings 3:3-14. The first record of King Solomon using his GOD-given wisdom is found in 1 Kings 3:16-28, where he rendered a perfect, just, and very wise judgment. Amen.

20. Although YHWH does not usually do anything without revealing His secrets (plans) to His servants the prophets, See Amos

3:7, He will, nevertheless, sometimes hide certain matters from them. See 2 Kings 4:27. Amen.

21.The Day and Hour of Christ's return is unknown to everyone, except the FATHER Himself. No man knows; the angels do not know, nor the Son Himself. See St. Mark 13:32-37.Amen.

22.No curse, sorcery, magic, or divination can touch or harm the children of Jacob (Israel) and Abraham (the father of the faithful and the Friend of ELOHIM). It has absolutely no power against us. See Numbers 23:23. Amen. Moreover, a "causeless" curse will not work against any innocent person. See Proverbs 26:2. Amen.

23.Whoever preaches the Gospel must include the woman who Anointed YAHUSHUA . This shall be done as a memorial unto her. See St. Matthew 26:6-13. Amen.

24.Hell fire is eternal: It cannot be quenched. See St. Mark 9:43-48 + Revelation 20:10. Amen.

25.The "mark of the beast" is the number 666. Although some may play around with that number, and some may even get it tattooed on their body, they will receive the consequences of that action. See Revelation 13:16-18; 14:9-11. Amen. Furthermore, Revelation 19:20 makes known to us: "And the beast was taken, and with him the false prophet who wrought miracles before him, with which he deceived them who received the 'mark of the beast', and those who worshipped his image. They both were cast alive into a lake of fire burning with brimstone." Amen.

26.The end result of ELOHIM's three chief enemies: the devil (Satan), the false prophet, and the beast, is made known in Revelation 20:10, "And the devil who deceived them was cast into the lake of fire and brimstone, where the beast and false prophet are, and shall be tormented day and night for ever and ever." Amen. Thus,

EL SHADDAI's victory will reach its climax; for the Holy Scriptures cannot be broken. See St. John 10:35. Amen.

27.The two scariest Verses in the Holy Bible: Revelation 20:15 and Hebrews 10:31. Amen.

28.John the Baptist is the greatest person ever born of a woman (with a human father); and he was Elijah the Prophet in the spirit. See St. Matthew 11:11,14. Amen

29.Not everyone who is called is chosen. See St. Matthew 20:16; 22:14. Amen.

30.According to the will of ELOHIM, those who are first now will be last, and those who are last now will be first. See St. Matthew 20:16. Amen.

31.ELOHIM created everything by His Word, YAHUSHUA Messiah. See St. John 1:1-4 + Genesis 1:3-26 + Ephesians 3:9 + 1 John 5:7 (KJV). Amen.

32.ELOHIM hates divorce and does not approve of it for any reason except sexual immorality/fornication, which is adultery. See Malachi 2:15-16 + St. Matthew 5:31-32; 19:4-9. Amen.

33.We, EL's children, His saints and servants, are called by our FATHER's Name. See 2 Chronicles 7:14 + Jeremiah 14:9; 15:16. Amen.

34.True circumcision is not "external" or of the "flesh", but rather "internal" and of the "heart" (by the Spirit). Thus, a "Jew" is not one that is merely Jewish outwardly, but inwardly, having a circumcised "heart", and worships ELOHIM in "Spirit" and in "Truth". Amen. See St. John 4:24 + Romans 2:28-29 + Philippians 3:3 + Revelation 2:9 + Colossians 2:11-13. Amen.

35.There is a steadfast Law which even ELOHIM Himself does not pardon, and that is the Law of Sowing and Reaping. See Galatians 6:7-8. Amen. We reap what we sow, whether good or bad. You do good, good come back on you; you do bad, bad come back on you. For if you plant apple seeds, you will get apples, not oranges or grapes or any other fruit. Amen.

36.Those who exalt themselves will be brought low (abased), and those who humble themselves will be exalted (lifted up). See Ezekiel 21:26 + St. Matthew 23:12. Amen.

37.For a glimpse into what Judgment Day will be like, see St. Matthew 25:31-46. Amen.

38.Sometimes YAH will command us to "not" pray for a specific person or people. See Jeremiah 7:16 + 14:11 + 1 John 5:16. Amen.

39.With ELOHIM, one day is as a thousand years, and a thousand years as one day. See 2 Peter 3:8. Amen.

40.Perhaps the greatest mystery and revelation in the whole Holy Bible is the Truth of "who JESUS Christ really is?" Well, to sum it all up: JESUS (YAHUSHUA) is GOD (YAHWEH); for while on earth He was "One" with Him, how much so now that He has returned back to the FATHER in heaven. This "Oneness" is evidenced in the accumulative revelation throughout the entire Bible, similar to how the sunlight and the heat of the sun is one with the sun. It is clearly seen in JESUS' Words, Teachings, Healings, Authoritative Living (i.e. demanding spirits and demons and even the weather and sea, and their obedience to Him), and His perfection in His ways, actions, speech, and life in general. Also, it is evidenced by His Sacred Name in Hebrew (His race/nationality and the language He spoke), which is "YAHUSHUA". You see the "YAH" in His Name, which means "the LORD"; and even in His

English Sacred Names "JESUS", which means "JEHOVAH Saves" or "IMMANU'EL" or "EMMANU'EL", which literally means "GOD with us" or "EL with us" (ELOHIM with us). Moreover, you notice in the Holy Bible that JESUS' Name is in all caps (as given by the holy angel in St. Matthew 1:21-25), and only GOD Names are in all caps, thus revealing the Deity of JESUS Christ the Messiah. The discernment is that JESUS (YAHUSHUA) was ELOHIM (YAHWEH) manifested in the "flesh", although YHWH essence is "Spirit". See St. John 4:24. Amen. Thus, JESUS' Name literally means "GOD dwelling amongst us in the flesh" and another definition would be "GOD, the Word, coming to us with flesh to save us". Wherefore, when ELOHIM's Name is spelled "YHWH" or "YAHWEH" or "JEHOVAH", He is operating in His Original Most Holy and Sacred state; and when ELOHIM's Name is spelled "JESUS" or "YAHUSHUA" or "YESHUA" or "I/EMMANU'EL", He is operating as the Son or with flesh, as when He dwells on earth with us humans. Nevertheless, His Name change does not take away from the Truth that He is always/all ways Perfect, Holy, Sacred, and Divine. See St. Matthew 1:21-25 (KJV) + Isaiah 7:14; 9:6 + 1 Timothy 3:16 + St. John 1:1,14; 10:30. Amen.

41.One of the saddest Verses in the Holy Bible is found in Jeremiah 7:34 (The Book of the weeping Prophet). Amen.

42.The two most scariest Verses in the Holy Bible for unbelievers and impenitent sinners are Hebrews 10:31 (which denotes that no one can save you once you fall into the Hands of the Living ELOHIM), and Revelation 20:15 (which reveals that those whose names are not written in the Book of Life will be cast into the lake of fire (see also Revelation 21:8). Amen. The Bible is clear throughout that there are only two destinations awaiting all souls: Heaven, or hell. Amen.

43. The most comforting Verse in the Holy Bible is Revelation 21:7. Amen.

44. Those who disdain the Law or turn away their ear from hearing it, bring upon themselves a curse: for even their prayers are an abomination. See Proverbs 28:9. Amen. Even this goes back to the Law of Sowing and Reaping, because GOD, in essence, is saying "you're not listening to me, so I AM not listening to you. Remember when the hypocrites posed a question to JESUS, and JESUS in turn replied, "if you answer my question, I will answer yours." However, when they refused to give an answer, JESUS said "neither will I tell you…" Amen.

45. JESUS Christ is the King of kings and the Lord of lords. Amen. See 1 Timothy 6:14-16 + Revelation 17:14; 19:16. Amen.

46. One of the main reasons for Christ's first coming and manifestation is to "destroy the works of the devil". See 1 John 3:8 Amen. Another reason is that we may have "life and life more abundantly". See St. John 10:10. Amen. For further study on this subject, see 1 John 3:5 + St. Luke 4:43 + St. Matthew 5:17-19 (to fulfill the Law of EL). Amen.

47. In order to receive Eternal Life and become immortal, one must be "in Christ". For Christ alone, in ELOHIM, has Immortality, and Christ alone is the Giver of Eternal Life. See 1 Timothy 6:16 + 1 John 5:11-13,20. Amen.

48. Everyone have received a gift. See 1 Peter 4:4:10. Amen.

49. In 1st Corinthians 15:45-48, it is referring to "two Adams", one from the earth, earthly; the other from heaven, heavenly (the Lord). It is this mystery, that JESUS, "the Lord from heaven", referred to being the "Son of Man (Adam)", which discerningly means the "Son of Himself (GOD)" or the "Son of the Lord of heaven", which still means that He was in essence proclaiming that

He was the Son of Himself, because He was the "Lord GOD from heaven". The name "Adam" literally means "Man". For context, see specifically 1 Corinthians 15:45-48. Amen.

50. Salvation for our souls is a result of our "faith", which includes "works" and "obedience": for faith without works is dead! Although being "saved" is a free gift from ELOHIM, we still must "receive" it by faith; and faith without works is dead. For every instance in the Holy Bible where someone is commended for "having faith", they partook of some kind of "work" to show that they had faith. (For many examples of this see Hebrews Chapter 11). Amen. These "works", however, is quite different from the works of people doing things (works) just to appear righteous in the sight of others. For we do not do good works to "be" righteous; we do good works because we "are" righteous, and thus, we know no other way to live but righteously. We do not do righteous works to "earn" our salvation, but rather we do righteous works "because" of our salvation, and it is these "works" that differentiate between the saved and the unsaved. You tell a tree by the fruit that it bears. If someone proclaims that they are "saved", but producing fruits of being "unsaved", say, lying, cheating, smoking, drunkenness, fornication, etc., it shows that that person is not saved. For in life, everything we do is a "work", and it is either a "good work" or a "bad work". When Apostle Paul stated that we are not saved "by works" lest any man shall "boast", he was, in essence, saying that we do not do good works to be saved and boast about it, but rather when we do good works we do it in humility "because" we are saved, and thus, the good works are a natural product (fruit) of our salvation. For if this was not so, he would not have commanded us to "work out" our "own" salvation with fear and trembling, which shows some "working" involved with keeping our salvation. See Philippians 2:12. Amen. The saying of "once saved, always saved"

is a lie! For if a man get or become saved today, and many years from now, he rejects GOD, and he becomes a Satan worshipper, he has lost his salvation! And he's going to hell! For more clarity on Salvation and being saved, see 1 Peter 1:9 + Ephesians 2:8-9 + St. James 2:14-26 (in reference to "faith without works is dead"). Amen.

51. The first mention of "salvation" is found in Genesis 49:18. Amen.

52. Not all "believers" will enter into the kingdom of heaven. There are some requirements that YAHUSHUA Christ Himself specifically outlined for us that must be met before one can inherit or enter the kingdom of heaven. Some are as follows; (1) Must go through Christ, who is "The Way" there. This means believing in Him as the Son of EL, and receiving and obeying His teachings. See St. John 14:6. Amen. (2) You must be "born again" of "water and the Spirit". See St. John 3:3,5. Amen. (3) You must "do the will of ELOHIM". See St. Matthew 7:21. Amen. And (4) Your righteousness must exceed the righteousness of the scribes and Pharisees. See St. Matthew 5:20 + Acts 14:22. Amen.

53. Our souls are purified by obedience to the Truth through the Spirit. See 1 Peter 1:22. Amen.

54. The "stars" of heaven can "fight". The stars of heaven sometimes means "angels" of heaven. See Judges 5:20 + Revelation 9:1-2. Amen. See also Revelation 22:16 (where JESUS Himself is a "Star", specifically "the Bright and Morning Star"). Amen.

55. ELOHIM (GOD) is LOVE: See 1 John 4:8,16; ELOHIM is Light: See 1 John 1:5; ELOHIM is a Spirit: See St. John 4:24; ELOHIM is a "Consuming Fire": See Hebrews 12:29. Amen.

56. Without faith you cannot please ELOHIM, it is "impossible". See Hebrews 11:6. Amen.

57. Those who are in the flesh cannot please ELOHIM. See Romans 8:8. Amen.

58. We understand with our "heart". See St. Matthew 13:15. Amen.

59. The issues (experiences) of life comes out of our "heart". See Proverbs 4:23. Amen.

60. Not only does joy brighten us up (literally), but so does wisdom, which makes our face shine (literally). See Ecclesiastes 8:1 + Exodus 34:29-30. Amen.

61. The world will come to an end. See St. Matthew 13:39-40; 28:19-20. Amen.

62. The greatest thing we can desire and ask the FATHER for is wisdom. See Proverbs 8:11. Amen.

63. There are two kinds of "dead": the literal dead and those who are spiritually or mentally dead even while still living physically. See St. Matthew 8:21-22. Amen.

64. Even the devils and demons oftentimes possess more faith and awareness of GOD and His Christ than many professed "believers". This is evidenced by the truth that many so-called believers of JESUS' day did not recognize Him as the Messiah, while devils did and confessed Him the "Son of GOD". See St. Matthew 8:28-29. (Compare St. James 2:19). Amen.

65. The reason there is so much evil and corruption in the world is because of the state of man's "heart". Men like to blame the devil, but if men hearts were pure, men would be able to resist the devil and overcome his temptations. See St. Matthew 15:18-20; (compare Jeremiah 17:9 + Proverbs 4:23). Amen.

66.How to be great in the kingdom of heaven: Do and teach the Word (Commandments) of YHWH ELOHIM. See St. Matthew 5:19. Amen. So the keys here are: (1) Knowledge and (2) Obedience. Knowledge of the Word, in order to do it (obey) and teach it. Obedience to the Word, because one can know the Word and still choose not to do it. Thus, the obedience factor must be done "willingly" to make one a great person. Amen.

67.The greatest Commandment that IMMANU'EL gave is that we be "perfect" as our FATHER in heaven is perfect. See St. Matthew 5:48. Amen. This Commandment mostly has to do with being perfect "in LOVE", because "perfect LOVE cast out all fear". See 1 John 4:18. Amen.

68.JESUS confirmed more than once that He is indeed Christ, the Messiah. See St. Matthew 16:16-17; 22:42. Amen.

69.The greatest mystery and revelation about YAHUSHUA Messiah (JESUS Christ) is that He came as "YHWH ELOHIM" (GOD) in the flesh. Hence, ELOHIM with flesh (or "with us") is IMMANU'EL (YAHUSHUA/JESUS), and ELOHIM without flesh, as Pure Spirit is "YHWH ELOHIM". Since GOD cannot die, He had to take on the nature of the "Son of GOD" with a human body in order to die, rise, and reconcile His creation and creatures back unto Himself. See 1 Timothy 3:16 + St. John 1:1,14; 10:30; 14:9 + 1 John 5:7 (KJV). Amen.

70.All of the greatest Commandments have to do with "LOVE": Loving ELOHIM, and Loving others as ourselves. See Deuteronomy 6:4-5 + St. Matthew 22:37-40 + St. John 15:12. Amen.

71.ELOHIM chose the people who were "fewest" in number (the minority), and who were once considered "not a people" at all, to be His holy people. See Deuteronomy 7:6-7 + 1 Peter 2:9-10. Amen.

72.There is a real creature called "dragon". See Psalms 91:13. This Verse reveals that it is s serpent or some kind of snake. See also Revelation 12:3. Amen.

73.Quite ironically, the clouds of heaven comes from the earth; for ELOHIM makes the clouds "'ascend' from the remote parts of the 'earth'". "Ascend" means "rise"; thus, they rise from the earth and ascend into heaven, and they are the dust of YHWH's Feet. See Jeremiah 51:16 + Nahum 1:3. Amen.

74.The HOLY TRINITY (The Three that are ONE) appeared to Abram in Genesis Chapter 18. See also 1 John 5:7 (KJV) + Genesis 1:26. Amen. Also, from the context of Genesis 18 we perceive that ELOHIM knows even what we do "within" ourselves. For Sarah did not laugh aloud, but rather "inwardly", yet YHWH knew she laughed. See specifically Verses 10-15. Amen.

75.ELOHIM can make creatures sleep a "perpetual sleep"; meaning never awaking again, an everlasting or continuous sleep. See Jeremiah 51:39 + St. Matthew 19:26. Amen.

76.EL has appointed and given certain angels dominion and authority over specific creations and locations, i.e. the angel of the waters, of the fire, etc. See Revelation 9:11; 14:18; 16:5. Amen.

77.Stars are "beings" that can think and function, insomuch that a "star" is called "him" in Revelation, and to him was given the key to the bottomless pit. See Revelation 9:1. Amen.

78.JESUS' first Words as a Minister ministering (preaching) to a large crowd were "Blessed". Thus, Christ came to bless: for He is the Living Word, and His first Words to the general public was a blessing. And it also shows how much He cares for the poor and needy, since His first address addressed them. See "The Beatitudes" in St. Matthew 5:3-12. Amen.

79. The HOLY SPIRIT (HOLY GHOST) is GOD (ELOHIM). See Acts 5:3-4 + 1 John 5:7 (KJV) + St. John 4:24. Amen.

80. YHWH ELOHIM can put into His creatures' hearts to fulfill His will, and to agree to it. See Revelation 17:17. Amen.

81. We find the LORD's Name "JEHOVAH" ("YAHWEH or YHWH" in Hebrew) in Isaiah 12:2 (KJV) + Exodus 3:14-15 ("I AM THAT I AM/ADONAI ELOHIM"); 6:3 + Psalm 83:18. Amen.

82. The enemies of ELOHIM are those who love the world and the things that are in the world. See 1 John 2:15-17 + St. James 4:4. Amen.

83. LOVE is actually more Loving than it is Loved. In other words, LOVE LOVES more than it is Loved. Amen. See 1 Corinthians Chapter 13 + St. John 15:13. Amen.

84. Hell is referred to as "her". See Isaiah 5:14. Amen.

85. One day with JEHOVAH is as a thousand years, and a thousand years as one day. See 2 Peter 3:8. Amen.

86. Many Bible scholars and Theologians believe that the Book of Job was written before any of the other Books of the Holy Bible, even before Genesis. Nevertheless, this belief has not been proven absolutely. However, what has been proven is that Job was a Black-skinned man. See Job 30:30 (KJV). Amen.

87. It should be noted that JESUS said "ascending" first when describing how the angels of ELOHIM would be interacting with Him. This reveals that the kingdom of ELOHIM is indeed "within" us (who are in Christ), and that the angels were first coming out of YAHUSHUA (ascending), then coming back upon Him (descending) while He walked the face of the earth. See St. John 1:51; 3:13 + St. Luke 17:21. Amen.

88. The FATHER in heaven gives His children His Spirit, albeit by measure; nevertheless, He gives His only "begotten" Son, the Messiah Christ, His Spirit without measure (meaning fully). Amen. See St. John 3:34 (KJV) + Colossians 2:9. Amen.

89. The literal fruit that Adam and Eve ate may have been the "sour grape". Notwithstanding, the deeper meaning of that fruit most likely was "information" that was forbidden them, knowledge that the CREATOR ELOHIM did not desire or will for them to possess or partake of because it would corrupt their innocence and purity. See Jeremiah 31:30. Amen. For some of the deeper meanings of "fruit", see Galatians 5:22-23 + St. Matthew 7:16-20 + St. Luke 6:43-45. Amen.

90. ELOHIM is the GOD of all spirits, souls, and flesh. As the CREATOR and MAKER of all, all belongeth unto Him and He has all Power to do as He will with them. Amen. See Jeremiah 32:27 + Hebrews 12:9 + Ezekiel 18:4 + St. Matthew 10:28 + Hebrews 10:31. Amen.

91. ELOHIM carried us "before" we were born. See Isaiah 46:4. Amen.

92. Christ specifically has a Law called "the Law of Christ", which teaches us to LOVE the FATHER and each other, and "bear one another's burdens…". See Galatians 6:2. Amen. This Law is one with "the Law of LOVE": for ELOHIM is LOVE, and Christ is One with ELOHIM, and therefore is LOVE. See St. John 10:30 + 1 John 4:7-21 + St. Matthew 22:37-40. Amen.

93. At least twice, JESUS said "whosoever has seen Me has seen the FATHER (who sent Me)", thus confirming His Deity. See St. John 12:45; 14:8-11. Amen. Moreover, He made known that "I and My FATHER are One". See St. John 10:30. Amen.

94.For some of the main reasons for JESUS Christ coming (manifesting Himself) in the flesh, see 1 John 3:8 + Hebrews 2:14-15 + 1 Timothy 1:15 + St. John 18:37. Amen.

95.No excuse for sin anymore: See St. John 15:22-24 + Hebrews 10:26-27. Amen.

96.We can do nothing without Christ, who is the Word, our CREATOR. Amen. See St. John 1:1-14 (specifically Verses 3 + 10) and 15:5. Amen.

97.St. John 15:6 is referring to Hell. Compare St. Matthew 13:40-42 + Revelation 20:15. Amen.

98.We must "through much tribulation" enter into the kingdom of heaven. See Acts 14:22. Amen. This Verse, and 2 Timothy 3:12 shows that inheriting or entering the kingdom of heaven is not easy. However, we can do all things through Christ who strengthens us; and with ELOHIM all things are possible. See Philippians 4:13 + St. Mark 10:27. Amen.

99.The revelation of 777 is in Revelation 5:6. Amen.

100.Christ the Messiah's Spirit always existed, even before He was born of flesh with a human body of the Virgin Mary and called JESUS. For He is the Lamb that was slain from the "foundation" of the world, predating the Old Testament and Moses' days. Amen See Exodus 17:6 + 1 Corinthians 10:4 + Numbers 20:8-11. Amen.

101.In Scripture, trees are sometimes symbolic for men and spirits. See Isaiah 61:3. Amen. Thus, the "forbidden tree" in Genesis could be figurative of Satan (that serpent of old), and "the fruit" thereof symbolic of the harmful information that he possessed (for he was Lucifer, who knew the heavenly knowledge of "good and evil" and was kicked out of heaven and cast down to the earth with it. Hence, harmful "information" that ELOHIM did not want nor will for His children to intake, digest, or partake of. See Genesis 3:1-19 + Ps. 1:3 + St. Matthew 7:15-20. Amen.

102.Souls are sold in Babylon. See Revelation 18:13. Nevertheless, all souls must answer to their CREATOR and OWNER. See Ezekiel 18:4. Amen.

103.All souls are ELOHIM's. See Ezekiel 18:4. Amen.

104.Death can "flee" from people. See Revelation 9:6. Amen.

105.For the Three that are ONE, see St. Matthew 28:19 + 1 John 5:7 (KJV). Amen.

106.JESUS also came to save those (and that) which were lost. See St. Matthew18:11. Amen.

107.JESUS was manifested to save His people from their sins, to take away our sins. See 1 John 3:5 + St. Matthew 1:21 + St. Luke 2:10-11. Amen.

108.YHWH ELOHIM's (the LORD GOD's) Word never returns unto Him void, but it accomplishes all that He sent it to accomplish, perfectly. See Isaiah 55:11. Amen.

109.In St. Matthew 18:34-35, King JESUS gives a scenario or ideology similar to that of "purgatory" or a "temporary" stay in hell until one's sins and wrongs are paid for (by the transgressor himself or herself). Compare Psalms 16:10 (KJV), where King David mentions that ELOHIM will not "leave" his soul in hell. This can have either two meanings: (1) There are "levels" to hell, and certain levels (or at least one) one can be released or freed from; or (2) David could have been referring to "hellish experiences". One, or both, of these explanations will have to suffice, because the Doctrine of the Holy Bible teaches that once a soul is cast into hell it remains in hell forever. See Revelation 20:10,15; 21:8. Amen.

110.The secret mystery of the HOLY TRINITY being ONE is revealed in that ELOHIM the FATHER/CREATOR is the HOLY SPIRIT and JESUS Christ is His Word (The Word). See 1 John 5:7 (KJV) + St. John 1:1,14; Acts 5:3-4 (in this specific Verse in Acts it makes clear that the HOLY SPIRIT is GOD, because it states "…why has Satan filled your heart to lie to the HOLY SPIRIT (or HOLY GHOST)…you have not lied to men, but to GOD." Thus, them that lied to the HOLY SPIRIT lied to ELOHIM who is the HOLY SPIRIT. See also St. John 4:24 and Genesis 1:2, both showing clearly that YHWH ELOHIM (the LORD GOD) is a SPIRIT, specifically the HOLY SPIRIT, as seen above in Acts and also in 1 John 5:7 (KJV). Moreover, YAHUSHUA Messiah's only FATHER is GOD the HOLY SPIRIT, see St. Matthew 1:18-20, where the Virgin was found with Child by the "HOLY SPIRIT". Amen.

111.The "righteousness" of the scribes and Pharisees is that they "taught" the Law and Word of EL, by they themselves did not "do" it or live it, which is hypocrisy. For if a man teaches that men should not smoke because it is a sin, yet he himself smoke, it shows that he is not practicing what he preaches, and thus, is a hypocrite. Hence, in order for our righteousness to exceed theirs, we must be "doers" of the Word also, not merely hearers or teachers of it. Amen. See St. Matthew 5;20 + St. James 1:22. Amen.

112.in St. John 17:3, IMMANU'EL said "And this is Eternal Life, that they might know You the only true 'EL', and YAHUSHUA Christ whom you have sent." Amen. Anyone who's acquainted with the Sacred Hebrew tongue/language and the Holy Scriptures in its Original Writing, knows that the CREATOR GOD Name is "ELOHIM" or "EL" (shortened version). See Genesis 1:1 in Hebrew Bible. Thus, "EL" (GOD) is 'E'ternal 'L'ife, and He and His Son IMMANU'EL Messiah (JESUS/YAHUSHUA Christ) is the sole Giver of Eternal Life. Amen. See St. John 14:6 + 1 John 2:25; 5:11-13,20. Amen.

113.ELOHIM has seven Spirits: His "HOLY SPIRIT" being the Highest and encompasses all of His Spirits as One. Amen. See Revelation 1:4 (compare 1 John 5:7 KJV, where the "HOLY SPIRIT" is the Spirit identified as GOD. Amen.

114.IMMANU'EL Christ (JESUS/YAHUSHUA Messiah) is "the Prince" of the kings of the earth; meaning, their "Ruler". See Revelation 1:5. Amen.

115. 'But I AM YHWH thy ELOHIM, that divided the sea, whose waves roared: YHWH of hosts is His Name." Amen. Hence, the CREATOR ELOHIM's Name is "YHWH", pronounced "YOD HAY WAW HAY" in the Hebrew tongue, and "YAHWEH" in English. See Isaiah 51:15. Amen.

116.Another of YAHWEH's great covenants with those of the earth, besides the sign of the rainbow in Genesis 9:8-17, is the blessing upon those who keep His Sabbath, specifically the blessing of giving them a name greater than of "sons and daughters". See Isaiah 56:2-7; 58:13-14. Amen.

117.When JESUS stated, "And I say also unto thee, that thou art Peter, and upon 'this' rock I will build my Church; and the gates of hell shall not prevail against it…." In St. Matthew 16:18, He was not specifically saying that He will build His Church upon "Peter" himself, but upon "the Truth" of St. Peter's confession that JESUS is indeed "the Christ (Messiah), the Son of the Living ELOHIM", as seen in the previous two Verses 16-17. Amen. Wherefore, He was making known that He would build His Church upon this "rock" (foundation) of "Truth", especially the Understanding of the Truth that He is the Messiah/Christ, the Son of the Living EL. See St. Matthew 16:16-18. Amen. Compare St. Matthew 7:24-29. Amen.

118.Prophets and Priests shall not divine or teach for pay. See Micah 3:11. Amen. Nevertheless, the people can voluntarily give "free will offerings" and gifts to their men and women of GOD. See Acts 4:35-37; 5:1-2. Amen. This money in turn shall be used mainly for the Church, helping the needy, fatherless/orphans, and widows. See the context in Verses 32-37 of Acts Chapter 4. Amen.

119.In Habakkuk 3:3 it states, "ELOHIM came from Teman, the HOLY ONE from mount Paran. Selah." Amen. "Teman" is s certain location, and it represents "the right side" and "the South", specifically by the land of Edom and Judah; and it is a place rich in wisdom. Compare Jeremiah 49:7. Amen.

120.All silver and gold are YAHWEH ELOHIM's. See Haggai 2:8. Amen.

121.All souls are ELOHIM's. See Ezekiel 18:4. Amen.

122.One of JESUS' other Names/Titles is "The BRANCH". See Zechariah 6:12. Amen.

123.It is impossible for ELOHIM to lie. See Hebrews 6:18 + Titus 1:2. Amen.

124.Christ is "Prince Messiah" (Messiah the Prince). Amen. See Daniel 9:25 (KJV or NKJV). Amen.

125.YHWH restores the youthfulness and strength of those who faithfully wait on Him in prayer. See Job 33:25-26 + Isaiah 40:30-31. Amen. And this "strength" comes from Christ, through whom believers can do "all things", according to the will of the MOST HIGH. See Philippians 4:13. Amen.

126.There are a few men of ELOHIM that either called down or made fire come down from heaven: Elijah the Prophet, see 1 Kings 1:10-12; King Solomon, see 2 Chronicles 7:1; and Moses the

Man of GOD, and Aaron the High Priest of EL, see Leviticus 9:23-24. Amen.

127.The Spirit of ELOHIM raised up Adonai (the Lord), and He will also raise us up (His faithful believers). See 1 Corinthians 6:14. Amen.

128.We are not to "love" sleep, although we shall get the proper amount of it, without overindulging or becoming lazy or slothful. See Proverbs 20:13; 3:24. Amen.

129.For a thorough exposure to much of the history of Israel, see Psalm 78. Amen.

130.The children of Israel provoked, tempted, and doubted YHWH. See Psalm 78:17-20,32,36-37,41. Amen.

131.Most of the children of Israel did not believe in YAHWEH ELOHIM nor trusted in His salvation. See Psalm 78:22,32,36-37,41. Amen. This shows that although it is instilled in "every" soul and spirit the "existence" of YAHWEH ELOHIM (which means everyone believes that there "is" an EL), not everyone believes "in" Him and in His unlimited Power, His willingness and perfect ability to protect, provide, deliver, accomplish any feat., etc. See St. James 2:19 + St. Matthew 19:26 + St. Mark 10:27 + St. Luke 1:37; 18:27 + Philippians 4:19. Amen.

132.Man did eat angels' food. See Psalm 78:25 + Exodus 16:1-5. Amen.

133.The "filling" spoken of by the Messiah Christ in His Sermon on the Mount (see St. Matthew 5:6) is the filling of the HOLY SPIRIT of JEHOVAH ELOHIM (YHWH). Amen. See St. John 7:37-39. Amen. Be filled with the HOLY GHOST. Amen.

134.The LORD ELOHIM calls men and women, and sometimes He literally calls us by name. This is called "a calling" or "your calling" or "my calling" from GOD (ELOHIM). Then He will reveal to you your office(s), if He hasn't already. See Acts 13:2 + Exodus 31:1-4 + 1 Samuel 3:4-10. Amen.

135. The Holy Sabbath is a "perpetual" covenant and statute (Law), and as such, shall be kept from generation to generation. See Exodus 31:16-17. Amen.

136. Although the other Commandments, Instructions and Teachings in the Holy Bible (the Word of GOD-YHWH ELOHIM) were written by the holy prophets, apostles, and other holy men of GOD as they were moved by the HOLY SPIRIT, the Ten Commandments, however, were written by ELOHIM Himself, with His own Finger. See Exodus 31:18 + 2 Peter 2:20-21 + 2 Timothy 3:16-17. Amen.

137. The Tabernacle of the congregation and the Ark was and is Anointed. See Exodus 30:25-29. Amen.

138. Since "Catholic" means "broad", and the like, Christ's definition of "the broad way" in St. Matthew 7:13-14 could include the "Broadway of New York" (a State of the United States of America that we all see has much corruption); and also the Catholic faith, especially considering some of their unscriptural doctrine, such as the Blessed Virgin Mary being the "Mother of GOD", some of them worshipping her and/or worshipping other "saints" or angels, or praying to them. The Blessed Virgin is the "Mother of the Son of GOD", not GOD Himself. For GOD (ELOHIM) is the FATHER and CREATOR of all: the First and the Last. Amen. There is no place in the Holy Scriptures that support the teaching or doctrine of worshipping anyone or anything except ELOHIM only (His SPIRIT- the HOLY SPIRIT), nor praying to anyone besides Him, nor praying in anyone's else's name besides JESUS/YAHUSHUA/YESHUA/IMMANU'EL. Even though

JESUS Christ promised believers that we can ask Him (JESUS) for something or to do something for us, and He will do it, He never taught us to worship Him, but the FATHER, nor pray to Him, but directly to the FATHER in His Name. The few instances where someone "worshipped" JESUS in the Holy Bible, JESUS Himself did not ask for it nor require it. And although He did not reprove them for doing so (like the holy angels reproved them), this merely shows that it is not utterly wrong to worship Him in the sense that He is One with GOD (ELOHIM) whom we worship, but the entirely correct worship is the worship of the "SPIRIT of YHWH ELOHIM; and since JESUS had flesh when He walked the face of the earth, He was not all Spirit, and we are not to worship flesh. Amen. For further study on this profound topic, see St. Matthew 6:9-13; 18:19 + St. John 4:22-24; 14:13-14; 17 (WC) + Revelation 19:10. Amen. In these Verses you will find that JESUS Himself worshipped ELOHIM and prayed to Him. Amen.

139.EL is sometimes called an "Angel" and even appears as such occasionally. Moreover, He shall utilize the Voice of the "Archangel" when He return and descend from heaven. See Genesis 48:15-16 + Exodus 3:1-6 + 1 Thessalonians 4:16. Amen. "The Archangel" most likely being Michael or Gabriel-both are now the Chief Archangels since Lucifer's fall, who was more of a "Cherubim" than an Angel or Archangel. See Ezekiel 28, specifically Verse 16. Amen.

140.Our "works" will be tested by fire. "Good works" will not be burned up and shall receive a reward. Evil, corrupt, and unjust works will be set ablaze. The fire that will test our works is the fire of EL SHADDAI's wrath and judgment: the fire that "goes before Him". See 1 Corinthians 3:13-14 + Psalm 97:2-3 + Exodus 32:10. Amen.

141.One can "become" a Jew, even if not born one. See Esther 8:17. Amen. And a real Jew is he or she who is one "inwardly", in heart and spirit, seeking to please GOD, not man. See Romans 2:29. Amen.

142.According to the Ancient Sacred Calendar (ASC), or the Hebrew/Jewish Calendar, the first month of the year is "March", and the last (or twelfth-because the Hebrew Calendar occasionally has thirteen months) is "February". Valentines Day, according to the American Calendar, is a Jewish Holyday, which the Jews have been celebrating (albeit usually with a different name and in accordance with the ASC) since the days of Esther and Mordecai. See Esther 8:17; 9:19. Amen. Furthermore, "Christmas Day", or the Day on which Christ's Birthday is celebrated, according to the ASC, is February 25th, or 26th if the sun had already set on the 25th, which marks a new day according to Hebrew/Jewish culture. Amen.

143.The test of Job ended when he (Job) prayed for his friends. When he chose to forgive them, by praying to ELOAH on their behalf, that they be forgiven for their ridicule, slander, and insults with which they attacked Job's character and innocence, it was at this point that Job ultimately passed the test, was restored, and received twice as much as he previously had. Thus, we see the power of forgiveness. Also, we see the truthfulness of JESUS' admonition: that if we forgive others, we ourselves will be forgiven of the FATHER, but if we do not forgive others, neither will our heavenly FATHER forgive us. See Job 42:10 + St. Matthew 6:14-15. Amen.

144.Wisdom has children. See St. Matthew 11:19. Amen.

145.ELOHIM (GOD) is a SPIRIT, and His SPIRIT is invisible. See ST. John 4:24 + Colossians 1:15. Amen.

146.Rightly dividing the Word of Truth: "Scripture"= "Scriptrue/Script True", meaning, it has or will come to pass. Thus, "Scriptures=Scriptruths/Script Truths. See 2 Timothy 2:15 + St. Matthew 5:17-18. Amen.

147.Leah, the mother of some of Jacob's (Israel's) children, was a kind of "seer"; for she said what she "perceived" (saw in the Spirit), and it was indeed actually what YAHWEH saw and showed (revealed) to her. See and compare Genesis 29:31and 29:32-35. Amen.

148.One of the greatest secrets ever is: LOVE is what makes one perfect; the greater one's capacity to LOVE, the more perfect one will be. LOVE is the presence of GOD dwelling in us, because remember that GOD is LOVE. Amen. See 1 John 4:7-21, spec. V. 16; 2 Timothy 1:7 + St. James 2:8 + 1 Peter 4:8 + Romans 13:10 + St. Mathhew 5:48; 22:36-40. Amen.

149.ELOHIM has given Christ children. See Hebrews 2:13. Amen. Thus, JESUS Christ the Messiah and Son of GOD has children. Amen.

150.ADONAI will return. See St. James 5:8 + Philippians 4:5 + 1 Thessalonians 4:15-17. Amen.

151.Although ELOHIM promised to never again destroy the earth by water, the world is being reserved for fire. See Genesis 9:8-17 + 2 Peter 3:7-12. Amen.

152.Every creature is created "good" by ELOHIM, but it is the creature(s) itself who chooses to go out and corrupt itself. See 1 Timothy 4:4-5. Amen. For even Lucifer was created good and perfect, until he chose to rebel against his CREATOR, and become Satan. EL ELYON said, "You was perfect in your ways from the day that you were created, till iniquity was found in you". See Ezekiel 28:12-15, spec. V. 15. Amen.

153.ELOHIM's Face cannot be seen by a man and that man live. He can only be seen by His angels and other heavenly hosts. Nevertheless, man can behold Him or "see Him" in His glory, which is really seeing His glory as a reflection or representation of Him, until man overcome the world and "be with Him"; then man will be able to see Him fully. See Exodus 33:20-23 + 2 Chronicles 7:14 + 1 John 4:12 + Revelation 21:3-4,7. Amen.

154.There is a Day of Visitation, in which YAHWEH visit the earth, thoroughly inspecting men and their works. See 1 Peter 2:11-12. Amen.

155.YHWH made His Name known to Abram (Abraham). See Genesis 15:7. Amen.

156.Satan binds people with infirmities, deformities, diseases, sicknesses, etc. See St. Matthew 15:22; 17:18 + St. Mark 6:13; 7:29-30 + St. Luke 8:2; 13:10-17. Amen.

157.Although it is JESUS and the FATHER EL who heals all diseases, it is one's "faith" that makes them whole and well. A person who prays for healing without faith will not see the same results as someone who has faith in JESUS' ability and power to heal and prays for healing with that belief. Wherefore, it is the "faith" that one has in the FATHER and in the Son that is the key to that person being healed and made whole. See St. Matthew 9:20-22; 14:36; 15:28 + St. Mark 5:34. Amen.

158.The serpent is the wisest of all animals that ELOHIM created. See Genesis 3:1 + St. Matthew 10:16. Amen.

159.Whosoever sees YAHUSHUA (JESUS/IMMANU'EL) sees the FATHER who sent Him. For JESUS was GOD in the flesh, as evidenced by His Life and His Name "IMMANU'EL", which literally means "GOD with us" (ELOHIM/EL with us). See St. John 12:45; 14:7-11 + St. Matthew 1:23. Amen.

160.In the last Day, JESUS Christ's Word will Judge all men and women who rejects Him. See St. John 12: 48; 15:22. Amen.

161.For us believers in Christ, anything we ask the LORD in His Name, He will do it. See St. John 14:13-14. Amen.

162.How the end will be: See 1 Corinthians 15:24-28. Amen.

163.Storms were named even in Apostle Paul's days. See Acts 27:14. Amen.

164.There are "two" Resurrections. See Revelation 20:5. Amen.

165.When you are in the will of EL, He will send His angel before you to prepare and make straight your way. For ELOHIM's angels protect and encamp around those who fear Him. See Exodus 33:2 + Psalm 34:7; 91:11-12. Amen.

166.Moses named the place where YAHWEH's Spirit dwelt and met with His people "The Tabernacle of the congregation". See Exodus 33:7-10 (KJV). (Compare Rev. 21:3). Amen.

167.Abraham is "the Friend of GOD", see St. James 2:23, Amen. Moses also is the Friend of GOD, and YHWH ELOHIM spoke with him Face to face as a man speaketh unto his friend. See Exodus 33:11. Amen.

168.Those who Love YAHWEH ELOHIM is known by Him. See 1 Corinthians 8:3 + Exodus 33:12-17. Amen.

169.The Hebrew Israelites (Jews) became officially consecrated and set apart from the other people of the earth when Moshay (Moses) asked for such and YAHWEH ELOHIM granted his request (because he found grace in YHWH's sight). See Exodus 33:15-17 + St. Matthew 7:11. Amen.

170.ELOHIM will be gracious to whom He will, and He will be merciful to whom He will. For ELOHIM is the MOST HIGH, and He does whatsoever He wants. See Exodus 33:19 + Psalms 50:12; 91:1. Amen.

171.Although EL SHADDAI has "appeared" to many people, especially holy men and women of EL, sometimes appearing in the form of an Angel or Man, or even through, in, or as Natural Elements, such as Fire and Water, and has spoken to His chosen ones (some He even spoke to "Face to face"), no one has ever seen, nor can see the Face of ELOHIM and live, except in Heaven. See 1 John 4:12 + Exodus 3:2-6; 33:11,20-23 + Romans 1:20-25. Amen.

172.One of the most ironic statements of YHWH ELOHIM in the Holy Bible is in Exodus 34:7, where He proclaims forgiveness of sins and mercy "for thousands", and yet in the same Verse He makes known that He will "by no means clear the guilty; visiting the iniquity of the fathers upon the children…." At first glance, one may assume this Verse to be contradictory, because everyone who commits sins are "guilty" right? However, the truth of the matter is that ELOHIM is proclaiming mercy and forgiveness to those who "repent", which means they feel godly sorrow for committing their sins, they confess their sins to GOD, they turn away from their sins, and renew their minds (changing their mind and behavior for the better and in accordance with the will of GOD). But JEHOVAH's wrath is upon them who refuse to repent. See Ezekiel 18:21-23 + 2 Chronicles 7:14 + 1 John 1:9 + Proverbs 28:13 + 2 Corinthians 7:10. Amen.

173.Not "money" itself, but rather "the love" of money is the root of all evil. This is not just dealing with loving literal money (cash, gold, etc.), but is more profoundly dealing with greed, overindulgence, jealousy, envy, pride, arrogance, being a lover of pleasure more than a Lover of GOD, etc. Even Lucifer falls into this category, although his initial greed was not for literal "money", but for power and position. Anytime someone is "money-hungry" or "covetous" (wanting something that's not theirs or wanting more than what ELOHIM has given them as their portion), it falls into the category of "loving money", which leads to envy and jealousy, which leads to all kinds of evil thinking and behavior (thus, the "root"). Moreover, when someone "loves" money, they will do all types of underhanded things to get it, such as killing the innocent for it, robbing, stealing, lying, cheating, etc., to get it. See 1 Timothy 6:9-12. Amen.

174. YHWH is the One who opens wombs, enabling women to conceive and bear children. See Genesis 29:31; 30:2 + Psalms 127:3. Amen.

175. The LORD will return. See St. James 5:8 + Philippians 4:5 + 1 Timothy 6:14 + 1 Thessalonians 4:13-17. Amen.

176. YAHUSHUA Messiah, the Son of YAHWEH, dwell in unapproachable Light, which no man has seen nor can see; for we see what happened when Saul (now Apostle Paul) tried to approach that unapproachable Light: he became blind. See 1 Timothy 6:16 + Acts 9:1-9; see also 1 John 1:5 + St. John 1:4-9; 8:12. Amen.

177. When we are not in the will of ELOHIM or around the people that He desires for us to be around, even the people we are around will be "pricks" in our eyes, and "thorns" in our side (or flesh). Also, ELOHIM Himself will allow a thorn in our flesh (He will allow a messenger of Satan to buffet or harass us) to keep us from pride, from being conceited, as we see with Apostle Paul after he received a deep revelation from the third Heaven. And the Lord will not immediately take away the thorn, but will wait for our humility, until we become humble. See Numbers 33:55 + 2 Corinthians 12:7. Amen.

178. For teachings specifically for men and women of GOD, see 1 Timothy 6:11-12. Amen.

179.Abraham is the father of all "believers", whether circumcised or uncircumcised. See Romans 4:11-12 + Galatians 3:7. Amen.

180.There are different kinds of wisdom. See St. James 3:13-17. Amen.

181.YHWH ELOHIM's Name as "JAH" or "YAH" appears even in English Holy Bibles. See Psalm 68:4 (KJV). Amen.

182.JESUS Christ cannot die again. See Romans 6:9-10 + 1 Peter 3:18. Amen.

183.We are to "yield" ourselves unto ELOHIM, which means surrender, submit, and give ourselves fully unto Him; and our members are to be "instruments of righteousness" unto Him, which means we are to let Him use us and our bodies completely, however He wills and chooses. See Romans 6:13 (compare Rom. 12:1-2). Amen.

184.It is "LOVE" that covers all sins. In other words, the more one Loves, the more one will be forgiven. See Proverbs 10:12 + 1 Peter 4:8. Amen.

185.The theme of 1 Corinthians Chapter 13 is not so much as us needing or having Love in only a "charitable" sense, since "feeding the poor", etc., are acts of charity, but more so needing and having "GOD", who is LOVE. For if we have ELOHIM (who is LOVE), we will naturally do Loving things, such as feeding the poor. Thus, "acts of Love" is not the literal profound message of this Chapter, but rather "knowing and having GOD" and having an intimate relationship with Him as our CREATOR and FATHER. If we do not accomplish this feat in our lifetime our whole life was wasted in futility, vanity, and worthlessness. See 1 Corinthians 13 + 1 John 4:7-21. Amen.

186. When YAHUSHUA Christ gave His disciples/apostles the HOLY GHOST, He also gave them the power to retain (preserve) or forgive the sins of others. See St. John 20:22-23. Amen.

187. The parable of the talents is about saving souls in general, not just saving your own soul, or being selfish. See St. Matthew 25:14-30. Amen.

188. Who will be the least and who will be the greatest in the kingdom of heaven? See St. Matthew 5:19. Amen.

189. Just as there are different levels of Heaven, with the third (or some scholars, theologians, and men of GOD says the seventh) being the highest and most pleasurable and blissful, there are also levels of hell, with the literal hell fire and brimstone being the lowest and most painful and tormenting. See 2 Corinthians 12:2 + Psalm 16:10 + Acts 2:27 + Revelation 20:10,15; 21:8. Amen.

190. There are three water baptisms spoken of in the Holy Bible: the baptism in Moses, the baptism of St. John the Baptist, and the baptism into the Lord JESUS Christ (in the Name of the FATHER, and of the Son, and of the HOLY SPIRIT). The last baptism suffice when it is done either of these three ways: (1) by literally saying "in the Name of the FATHER, and of the Son, and of the HOLY SPIRIT (or HOLY GHOST), with the person being baptized believing that this is the same FATHER, Son, and HOLY SPIRIT spoken of by JESUS (YAHUSHUA/IMMANU'EL/YESHUA); or (2) by saying "in the Name of JESUS Christ" only (His Name in English or Hebrew, or Greek, or whatever other language He accepts His Name in; or (3) by saying "in the Name of the Lord JESUS". All three of the methods of baptizing were performed with the permission and authority of JESUS Messiah Himself, either personally or through His holy apostles. See 1 Corinthians 10:1-2 + Acts 2:38; 19:3-6 + St. Matthew 28:19. Amen.

191. What is the reason why not everyone who says unto JESUS, 'Lord, Lord', and those claiming to have cast out devils and performed miracles in His Name shall not enter into the kingdom of heaven? The reasons can be many, but here are a short list with Scripture backing it: They did not do "the will of the heavenly FATHER", some may outright lie and say they did those miracles, but in all actuality they didn't, or if they did use the Lord's Name to do them, they still never developed an "intimate" relationship with Him, this is evidenced by Him dismissing them by proclaiming "I never 'knew' you", many of them will be false prophets and false apostles (deceivers), some may have been righteous for a while (and may have really done miracles in Adonai's Name) but then backslide or turned to evil (in Scripture this backsliding is called "returning to one's own vomit"), many of them were not faithful to the Adon (Lord) or didn't remain loyal to Him, and lastly for now, some were not ready when Christ the Messiah returned and appeared, they stop "watching and praying". See St. Matthew 7:21-25; 25:11-12; 26:41 = Ezekiel 33:18. Amen.

192. Christ, the Son of ELOHIM, will put all things under His Feet (Authority), and then He Himself will become subject to ELOHIM (The MOST HIGH), that ELOHIM (YHWH EL SHADDAI) may be ALL and ALL. Amen. See 1 Corinthians 15:24-28. Amen.

193. To shed illumination on the revelation and Truth that the "second Man" is the "LORD from Heaven" who came down and dwelt among us (IMMANU'EL), to show what He really meant when He proclaimed Himself "the Son of Man", it means that He is the Son of Himself (the Son of the LORD of Heaven); remember that He has no earthly father, He (the HOLY SPIRIT) Fathered Himself even when He walked the face of the earth clothed in flesh. See 1 Corinthians 15:47 (compare St. John 3:13). Amen.

194.If you depend on (lean to) your "own" understanding when studying, you are headed towards misinterpretation, and maybe even confusion and delusion. See Proverbs 3:5-7 Amen. Let the HOLY SPIRIT of ELOHIM (the Spirit of Truth) guide and lead you into all Truth. Amen.

195.Whosoever desires to be the greatest in a group shall become the most humble and be the servant of all. See St. Matthew 20:26-28. Amen.

196.The sun is called "him" in Revelation 16:8. Amen. And it is called "the Sun of Righteousness" in Malachi 4:2. (Compare Revelation 22:16). Amen.

197.The sun has "sight" and can see. See 2 Samuel 12:12. So this actually may be "the all-seeing Eye of the MOST HIGH in the sky). Amen.

198.JESUS' Birth was and is a benefit and blessing for "everyone", not just a select few. All who put their trust in JESUS Christ as their Adon and Savior and call upon His Name shall be saved. See St. Luke 2:10-11 + 1 John 2:2. Amen.

199.Where the Gentiles come from? See Genesis 10:5. Amen.

200.Moshae (Moses), the man of ELOHIM, instructed the Israelites to "circumcise the foreskin of your heart…", which means "stop being cruel, merciless, and heartless, but purify your heart". See Deuteronomy 10:16. Amen. (Compare Deuteronomy 10:16 + Romans 2:29 + Ezekiel 36:26 + St. Matthew 5:8. Amen.

201.Some of the ways we perceive that JESUS Christ came also to be an "Example" of how we should live, what we should do, and how "we" are to overcome the evil one are because (1) Christ and ELOHIM are One, and therefore neither can be tempted with evil, but nevertheless, Christ allowed Himself to be tempted to "show us" how to overcome temptation: with the Word of EL. See St. James 1:13 + St. Matthew 4:1-10. Amen. (2) Christ did not have to nor need to be baptized, but He did so to "fulfill all righteousness", and if He did it, we all need to do it. It showed His humility by Him submitting to another man to be baptized by him, thus showing and teaching us "by example" to be humble and submissive to our man of GOD, or whosoever GOD will for us to be submissive to. See St. Matthew 3:13-15 + St. John 3:3-8. Amen. For it is obvious that YAHUSHUA Christ (JESUS Messiah) did not need to be baptized for the same reasons as others, for He did not need remission of sins, because He never sinned; He didn't need to be baptized unto repentance, for He was completely perfect and sinless; and also He did not need to be "born-again", because He Himself is the "Prince of Life" (Originator, Author). See Acts 3:15 + 2 Corinthians 5:21 + 1 Peter 2:22. Amen.

202.The New King James Version (NKJV), and some other Versions of the Holy Bible omitted "as a prince" in Genesis 32:28, which is included in the only Authorized English Holy Bible, the King James Bible (KJV/King James Version). The inclusion of this title is significant because it reveals in what capacity Ya'aqob (Israel) gained his victory. Compare KJV + NKJV. Amen.

203.The children of YHWH ELOHIM (The MOST HIGH GOD) is "gods" (little gods). See Psalm 82, specifically Verse 6 + Exodus 22:28. Amen.

204.One must have the Spirit of EL to know the things of EL. See 1 Corinthians 2:11-12. Amen.

205.The difference between "seasons" and "times". See Genesis 1:14 + Acts 3:19,21; 17:30 + St. Luke 21:24 + Ephesians 1:10 + Ecclesiastes 3:1-8. Amen.

206.The Gentiles have a "will". See 1 Peter 4:3. Amen.

207.The devil has a "will". See 2 Timothy 2:26. Amen.

208.JEHOVAH does not look on the "outer" appearance of a man (as men do), but He looks at a man's "heart". See 1 Samuel 16:7 + Acts 13:22. Amen.

209.Though Jacob and Israel are the same person, YAHWEH sometimes distinguishes His address to him. See Deuteronomy 33:10 + Numbers 23:23. Amen. The reasons for this is that (1)Jacob is an "individual", while Israel is Jacob and all of his family as one, a "multitude" (all of Jacobs seed that came from his body); and (2)Israel is the "spiritual" name of Jacob that YAHWEH ELOHIM Himself gave him, as opposed to the name given him by his earthly parents. See Genesis 32:24-28. Amen.

210.ELOHIM raised up the Lord (Adon/Adonai) and will also raise us up (the believers and faithful ones). See 1 Corinthians 6:14. Amen.

211.Although we are to "do good works", and we will be rewarded for such, see 2 Timothy 3:16-17 + Revelation 22:12, we are not to trust in our works. For it is not our "works" that saves us, but the LORD. See Jeremiah 48:7 + Ephesians 2:8-9. Amen. For anyone who is saved will live righteous and do good works anyway, because that is the "fruit" of being saved. Those who are not producing those types of fruit are not saved at all. See St. Matthew 7:16-20; 15:8 + Isaiah 29:13. Amen.

212.The Word of ADONAI ELOHAI "grow and multiply". See Acts 12:24. Amen.

213.Prophet Elijah raised the dead, see 1 Kings 17:17-24; prophet Elisha raised the dead, twice, see 2 Kings 4:18-37; 13:21; Apostle Peter raised the dead, see Acts 9:36-43; Apostle Paul raised the dead, see Acts 20:7-12; and JESUS Christ raised many people from the dead individually, and collectively at His death, where many saints' tombs were opened and they came back to life and appeared to many. See St. Mark 5:21-43 + St. Luke 8:40-56 + St. John 11:1-44 + St. Matthew 9:18-26; 27:50-53 Amen.

214.ELOHIM made all with and through YESHUA Messiah (JESUS Christ), His Word. See Hebrews 1:1-2 + St. John 1:1-3. Amen.

215.Esther 8:17 shows that one can "become" a Jew; and Romans 2:25-26 teaches who and what is a "Jew" and how one can distinguish a real Jew from an imposter. Amen.

216.We are fearfully and wonderfully made. See Psalm 139:13-16. Amen.

217.People and places also have "spiritual names". See Revelation 11:8 + Genesis 32:28. Amen.

218.Where did the Gentiles come from? See Genesis 10:1-5. Amen.

219.ELOHIM often speaks of man and woman or men and women interchangeably: for His Words and Messages to men usually always include women, unless otherwise noted or He specifically exclude women. See Exodus 21:20-21 (KJV). Amen.

220.It is "blood" that cleanses and purifies things, now in these New Testament days it is specifically the Blood of Christ the Messiah (the Lamb of ELOHIM). For it is the Blood of JESUS YESHUA/YAHUSHUA that cleanses the penitent sinner from his sins, thus purifying him and making him a new creature in Christ. See Hebrews 9:22 + 2 Corinthians 5:17. Amen. Moreover, it is by the Blood of the Lamb (the Christ/Messiah of GOD MOST HIGH) that we overcome the evil one, and with our testimony. See Revelation 12:11. Amen.

221.Although ELOHIM is the Most Merciful, there comes a point when sin become intolerable to Him and when this point arrives, there is no longer any sacrifice for one's sins. This point comes when one comes to the realization of the Truth and rejects it and chooses to sin willfully. See Hebrews 10:26-31. Amen.

222.YHWH ELOHIM is the MOST HIGH and He Himself sometimes gives testimony and bears record. See Acts 13:22 + 1 John 5:7-12 + St. Matthew 3:17 + 2 Peter 1:17-18. Amen.

223.Christ is also called "the Just One", meaning perfect in righteousness and justice (fairness, especially in judgment). See Acts 22:14. Amen.

224.ELOHIM gave Christ JESUS the full measure of His SPIRIT. See St. John 3:34 + Colossians 1:19 (KJV). Amen.

225.Wisdom is a "Tree of Life". See Proverbs 3:18. Amen.

226.YAHWEH has a "secret counsel" in which He confides in His Anointed and shares with His servants and chosen ones. See Proverbs 3:32 + Amos 3:7. Amen.

227.Wisdom is "the Principal thing", meaning "Chief Teacher/Instructor", similar to how a principal is the head of all the teachers at a school or other learning institution. See Proverbs 4:7. Amen.

228.The Way of Wisdom. See Proverbs 4:11 (compare St. John 14:6, where JESUS Christ, who is the Wisdom of EL SHADDAI, illuminates the Truth that He is the Way to the FATHER). Amen.

229.In every instance where man or woman is called a "dog" in the Holy Bible it is in a derogatory and degrading sense. See Philippians 3:2 + St. Matthew 7:6; 15:26 + Revelation 22:15. Amen. The latter revealing that "dogs", and the like (the unclean/abominable), will be "outside" the Gate of Heaven; this means that dogs will not enter into nor inherit the kingdom of heaven. Amen.

230. Who are "the Circumcision"? We are, who worship ELOHIM in the Spirit, and rejoice in YAHUSHUA Messiah, and have no confidence in the flesh. See Philippians 3:3. Amen.

231. Similar to how Christ received glory from GOD the FATHER, King Solomon received glory from Christ. See St. Matthew 6:29. Amen. Even so, all believers and followers of Christ received glory in St. John 17, specifically Verses 10,22. Amen.

232. 40 days is the standard or usual amount of time that it takes to complete a great mission (or, in some cases, prepare for it), task, or reach a great goal. See the examples of JESUS, Moses, and Elijah in St. Matthew 4:2 + Exodus 24:48 + 1 Kings 19:8. Amen. Additionally, JESUS even remained 40 days on earth "after" His resurrection, showing Himself to His chosen ones. See Acts 1:1-3. Amen.

233. Those who die in Christ, their "works" follow them. See Revelation 14:13. Amen.

234. We are saved by the Grace of ELOHIM, through faith in Him and in His Son YESHUA Messiah. See Acts 15:11 + Romans 10:9 + Ephesians 2:8-9. Amen.

235. There is an angel that EL gave power over fire. See Revelation 14:18. Amen.

236. Those of us who are called by the Name of the LORD YAH EL. See Acts 15:14,17 + 2 Chronicles 7:14 + Jeremiah 15:16. Amen.

237. The total Verses of St. Matthew Chapters 5,6, and 7 (The Sermon on the Mount by JESUS Christ) is 111, symbolizing "perfection", as when you see certain numbers appearing together consecutively, as in 333 and 777. Amen.

238.For starters and babes in Christ, see 1 Peter 2:1-3 and Acts 15:28-29. Amen.

239.The HOLY GHOST is the SPIRIT of YHWH ELOHIM: He is the HOLY SPIRIT who speaks to, and sometimes through, His prophets, apostles, servants, etc. See Acts 28:25-27 + 2 Peter 1:21. Amen.

240.YHWH ELOHIM (The LORD GOD) knows our "mind" and "thoughts", even every one of them. See Ezekiel 11:5. Amen.

241.Hell reaches one through their "tongue", and then the tongue sets the rest of the body ablaze with the fire of hell and defileth one's whole being. See St. James 3:6. Amen. That's why it is so important to guard and perfect one's speech, not indulging in idle, profane, or foolish talk. For whosoever can control their tongue can control the rest of their being. See St. James 3:2. Amen.

242."The Word" is "the Word of Truth", which is "the Spirit of Truth", and the Spirit of Truth is the "HOLY SPIRIT", and the HOLY SPIRIT is GOD (ELOHIM). See Genesis 1:1-2 + St. John 1:1-3; 4:24; 14:17; 15:26 + 1 John 5:7 + Psalm 51:11; 119:43 + Ephesians 4:30. Amen.

243.No man knows the FATHER nor the Son, except to whom the Son reveals such. See St. Matthew 11:27. Amen.

244.The "Word" of JESUS Christ (who is The Word) makes "judgments" also, and the same will make the final judgment on all who rejects JESUS/YAHUSHUA/YESHUA. See St. John 12:48 (see also 1:1-3 and 1 John 5:7 KJV, for Christ's Oneness with ELOHIM). Compare 2 Corinthians 5:10. Amen.

245.One can "see" ELOHIM, albeit only under the right circumstances. See St. Matthew 5:8 + Exodus 24:10-11 + 1st John 3:6; 3rd John 11. Amen.

246.We must be sure that we are doing "the LORD's will" by reading, studying, and learning the Word of YAH ELOHIM and applying this knowledge to our everyday life. We must remember that there are other "wills" that's not of GOD; for the "Gentiles" have a will, and the "devil" has a will. See first Ephesians 5:17, then see 1 Peter 4:3 + 2 Timothy 2:26. Amen.

247."Seasons" are distinguished from "times", insomuch as seasons are usually and mostly relatable to the atmospheric nature and changes, such as the sun, moon, stars, and weather in general, see Genesis 1:14; while "Times" are akin to spiritual or mental states/matters, such as the "times of ignorance" (Acts 17:30), "times of the gentiles" (St. Luke 21:24); "times of refreshing" (Acts 3:19); "times of restitution" (Acts 3:21); and "the Dispensation of the fullness of Times" (Ephesians 1:10). See also Ecclesiastes 3:1-8. Amen.

248.ELOHIM created man and women in His own likeness and image. See Genesis 1:26-27. Amen.

249.Some demons can only be cast out by prayer + fasting. See St. Matthew 17:21. Amen.

250.ELOHIM is the CREATOR of all, and the FATHER of spirits, the OWNER of all souls, and the GOD of all flesh. Amen. See Genesis 1:1 ("ELOHIM" GOD's Name in Hebrew, see Hebrew Bible) + Hebrews 12:9 + Ezekiel 18:4 + Jeremiah 32:27. Amen.

251.ELOHIM is LOVE: See 1 John 4:8,16; ELOHIM is Light: See 1 John 1:5; ELOHIM is The WORD: See St. John 1:1-3 + 1 John 5:7 (KJV); ELOHIM is The HOLY SPIRIT (The HOLY GHOST): See 1 John 5:7 (KJV) + 1 John 4:24; ELOHIM is a "Consuming Fire": See Hebrews 12:29. Amen.

252.YHWH EL SHADDAI (The LORD GOD ALMIGHTY) desires that we be merciful one to another, and to seek to know Him "intimately". See Hosea 6:6 + 2 Timothy 2:15 + Micah 6:8 + St. Matthew 5:7. Amen. Moreover, St. James 2:13 teaches that the merciless will be judged without mercy: another incidence of one reaping what they have sown. Amen.

253. The "natural" man does not receive the things of the Spirit of ELOHIM, nor can he, because they are "spiritually" discerned. See 1 Corinthians 2:14. Amen.

254. True Christians are those who have "the Mind of Christ". Amen. See 1 Corinthians 2:15. Amen.

255. Hidden wisdom of ELOHIM. See 1 Corinthians 2:7. Amen.

256. EL KANNA = JEALOUS GOD. This Name of ELOHIM is found in Exodus 34:14. Amen.

257. Crying to ELOHIM is "strength", not weakness. See Hebrews 5:7. Amen. For even JESUS (IMMANU'EL) had to "learn" obedience, learn to refuse the evil and choose the good, and be "made" perfect. See Hebrews 5:8-9 + Isaiah 7:14-15. Amen.

258. The first thing that ELOHIM created was "Light". See Genesis 1:1-5. Compare St. John 1:4-10 + Colossians 1:15 + Romans 8:29. Amen. Please note that while JESUS Christ is called "the Firstborn" and "the begotten of the FATHER", He is the Son and the FATHER as One, and as such, He has no beginning; He always existed with GOD and is One with GOD; only His "physical body/flesh" has a beginning (for He is the Word of GOD that "became" flesh), but He, as GOD's Word, and His Spirit is Eternal. See 1 Peter 1:10-11, where Christ the Messiah's Spirit was even in the prophets of the Old Testament. Amen. See also 1 Corinthians 10:4 + Exodus 17 + Numbers 20, where Christ was the Rock that the Children of Israel drank from even in Moses' day. Amen.

259.YAHUSHUA must "open" our understanding in order for us to understand, comprehend, and perceive spiritual truths. See St. Luke 24:45 + St. Matthew 13:13-14. Amen.

260.The LORD's Name is revealed in Jeremiah 31:35. In the original Hebrew tongue/language, in which GOD spoke and in which the Holy Scriptures were written in, the Sacred Holy Name is "YHWH" or "YHVH" (known as "the Tetragrammaton"), which, in English is translated and pronounced "YAH"/"YAHWEH" or "JAH"/"JEHOVAH" or "I AM"/"I AM THAT I AM"/"I AM WHO I AM". See Exodus 3:14-15; 6:3 + Psalm 83:18 + Isaiah 12:2, and the Hebrew Version of Jeremiah 31:35. Amen.

261.It is the work of the HOLY GHOST of putting His Laws into our hearts and writing them in our minds. See Hebrews 10:15-16. Amen.

262.People shall not strive (fight) against a priest. See Hosea 4:4. Amen. Moreover, the Priesthood and the position of High Priest are authoritative positions of rulership and are not to be disrespected. See Acts 23:5 + Exodus 22:28 + 1 Peter 2:13-15. Amen.

263.Apostle Paul was not only an Apostle, but also a Preacher, Teacher, Miracle Worker, and Healer. See 1 Timothy 2:7 + Acts 19:11-12. Amen. Furthermore, he spoke in "tongues" more than all the others of his day. See 1 Corinthians 14:18. Amen.

264.The HOLY SPIRIT calls and separates (sanctifies, sets apart, and ordains) people to do His work. See Acts 13:2. Amen.

265.Man was formed (created) first, then woman. See 2 Timothy 2:13 + Genesis 1:26-27; 2:7,18,21-24. Amen.

266.JESUS and the FATHER GOD are "One", meaning that both their Spirits are One and the same; similar how a man and his own spirit are one and the same: (his body and spirit). See St. John

10:30. Amen. ELOHIM is a "Three in One" Being: The FATHER, The WORD, and The HOLY GHOST (HOLY SPIRIT). And because He made us in His image and likeness, we too are threefold beings: Body (exterior/flesh), Soul (mind, feelings/emotions, and Spirit (true essence/being/existence). Hence, JESUS Christ is "the FATHER" when He is wholly Spirit, but whenever He takes on "flesh" He becomes "the Son", because GOD the FATHER is all SPIRIT with no flesh. Therefore, anyone who has "flesh" cannot be GOD nor claim to be, because GOD has no flesh; the highest dimension that flesh can take on is "the Son of GOD" or "the Incarnate 'of' GOD". When JESUS revealed that "whosoever has seen Me has seen the FATHER", He was referring to "GOD in Him/GOD's SPIRIT which was dwelling in His Body, which was manifest through His LOVE, perfect virtuous Life, miracles that no one else did, Teachings, Authority, etc."; that's why He concluded the proclamation with, "Do you not believe that the FATHER is "in Me" and "I in the FATHER". See St. John 14:7-11 + Revelation 19:10. Amen.

267.ELOHIM, the One and Only True Living God, had to make, or "express", Himself in and as Three Beings: The FATHER, The Son, and The HOLY GHOST, in order to do what GOD in His purest form of existence could not do: die; and also to make a way for repentant sinners to enter into His Presence in the kingdom of Heaven. The insight into this is that ELOHIM is a SPIRIT that cannot die. Therefore, He made Himself a "human Body" (that can die). Wherefore, He made Himself into a Man and become "The Son", hence, "The Son of Man", or in other words, decoded: "The Son of Himself" (The Man/Lord from Heaven, see 1 Corinthians 15:47. Amen). This "Man" who was "the Lord GOD from heaven with flesh" was, and is, YESHUA Messiah/YAHUSHUA Christ/ JESUS the Nazarene), who died for the sins of the world and resurrected for the forgiveness and reconciliation of all who places their trust in Him and His sacrificial atonement and repent. The Third Being is also "One" with the other Two, and this is "HOLY SPIRIT", which is GOD (ELOHIM), and known throughout the Holy Bible as "the Spirit of GOD/ELOHIM". He is perhaps the most mysterious of the Three, but upon thorough investigation of who He really is, one will see that He is actually "GOD" (YHWH ELOHIM), because GOD is "Holy" and He is a "Spirit" = the "HOLY SPIRIT". See Leviticus 11:44; 19:2 + 1 Peter 1:16 + St. John 4:24 + Genesis 1:2 + Ephesians 4:30. Amen. For He is the One responsible for the "working" and bringing about of the "Perfect Sacrifice" of His Son YAHUSHUA JESUS, and His role in all of it is what made this whole "transition", i.e., JESUS' Birth, Life on earth, His death, and resurrection "perfect" and complete and in perfect agreement and harmony with the "Holy Scriptures". Amen. See 1 Timothy 3:16 + St. Luke 1:35 + St. Matthew 1:20-25 + Acts 10:38 + 2 Corinthians 5:21 + 1 John 5:7 (KJV). Amen.

268.YHWH ELOHIM created everything, but that doesn't mean that He is "in" everything, nor is He. See 1 Kings 19:11-13. Amen.

269."Things" are not always "materialistic" in nature, or "possessive" in fact, or even "seen" according to the natural eye; some "things" are "spiritual things" (realties and qualities, such as LOVE, a wife, wisdom, Laws, etc.). See Proverbs 18:22 + Romans 8:28 + Deuteronomy 30:1 (KJV). Amen.

270.The world cannot see Christ: for indeed He is too Holy for their sight, and His Light is too bright for their darkness. Similar to turning on a light in a darkened room and the darkness flee and cannot remain to see the light, so it is with Christ the Messiah compared to this evil dark world. Notwithstanding, we, the siblings of Christ who are made into His image and members of His Body, can see Him. Moreover, we (believers) live because He lives, and upon His return in glory, us saints will appear in glory with Him. See 1 Timothy 6:13-16 + St. John 1:4-10; 14:19 + Romans 8:29 + 1 John 1:5 + Colossians 3:4. Amen.

271.Every believer that Loves JESUS Christ by keeping His Commandments and consistently obeying Him, is made One with Him and the FATHER (the HOLY GHOST), hence, becoming a "Holy Three" or "Holy Trinity". See St. John 14:20-21. Amen. Moreover, when you have the Word dwelling in you, and you are perfectly obedient to the Word, you "become" the 'Word with flesh'. See Colossians 3:16 + St. John 15:7. Amen.

272.The appearance of Christ and EL SHADDAI is revealed in Revelation 1:8,13-16; 4:2-3 + Daniel 7:9. Amen.

273.The whole Chapter 17 of St. John is JESUS' prayer to the FATHER, especially on behalf of His disciples (followers) and those who will believe on account of the words and testimony of His disciples. See St. John 17 (WC). Amen.

274.In St. John 17:2-3, JESUS revealed one of the secrets of the FATHER ELOHIM's Name. GOD's Name in Hebrew is "ELOHIM" or "EL", which also means "'E'ternal 'L'ife", and the Giver of such. "EL" also means "'E'LOHIM 'L'OVE", because ELOHIM (GOD) is LOVE. Amen. See 1 John 4:8,16 + St. John 17:2-3. Amen.

275.There is more than one heaven (levels). See 2 Corinthians 12:2-4. See also Genesis 1:1, where the NKJV and the ESV and some other Versions has "heavens". Amen.

276.There are also "levels" of hell; the lowest being the literal "lake of fire and brimstone"; another being the "bottomless pit"; another being "sheol"; another being "hades"; and the least (but still tormenting and painful) is a "state of misery, pain, and/or suffering" while living on earth. See Deuteronomy 32:22 (KJV) + Psalm 16:10 (NKJV) + St. Matthew 11:23 + St. Luke 16:23 + Revelation 1:18 (Christ the Messiah has the Keys to all of hell's departments (levels) and of death); and the following Verses refer to the worst level or "lowest" hell (the lake which burneth with fire and brimstone): See Revelation 20:14,15; 21:8. Amen.

277.ELOHIM took Moses, who was the most "humble/meek" man on earth (humble and meek meaning "lowly" and operating in humility), and made him "like EL" (like GOD the MOST HIGH). Now that shows you the power of humility! See Numbers 12:3 + 1 Peter 5:5 + St. James 4:8 + St. Matthew 23:12. Amen.

278.We will be judged for not only our "works", but for all three: our "works", "deeds", and "words". Our "deeds" being our "motives and intentions" behind the works and words; these "deeds" are "seeds" (deed-seeds) that Christ can see in our hearts to make just judgments. See St. Matthew 12:36-37 + Romans 14:10-12 + Jeremiah 17:10 + Revelation 20:12-15 + Proverbs 20:27 + Hebrews 4:12 + 1 Corinthians 4:5 + 2 Corinthians 5:10. Amen.

279.In Revelation 5:6 it speaks about the 7 Horns (of the Lamb of EL), the 7 Eyes, and the 7 Spirits of ELOHIM. The Seven "Horns" symbolize complete and perfect Power/Might (All-Powerful, Almighty, Omnipotent); the Seven "Eyes" symbolize complete and perfect "Sight/Vision" (Wisdom, Understanding, Knowledge: All-Seeing, All-Wise, All-Knowing/"Omniscient"); the Seven "Spirits" are manifestation of YHWH ELOHIM's Highest SPIRIT, which is His "HOLY SPIRIT", they are as follows: (1)The SPIRIT of The LORD; (2)the Spirit of Wisdom; (3)the Spirit of Understanding; (4)the Spirit of Counsel; (5)the Spirit of Might; (6)the Spirit of Knowledge; and (7)the Spirit of the fear of The LORD. See Isaiah 11:1-3. Amen. For further study on this, and on how although EL has many Spirits, He is One nevertheless, and also for a more thorough illumination on the Power of EL SHADDAI, See Revelation 4:5 + Psalm 139:8 + Deuteronomy 6:4 + 1 John 5:7 (KJV) + Isaiah 45:5-7 + Genesis 1:26-27 (where ELOHIM spoke to Himself, albeit in "plural" terms. Moreover, Since ELOHIM is the CREATOR of all, He can choose to be whatsoever He desire; this is evidenced by His very Name "ELOHIM", which is both singular and plural). Amen.

280. The "Lamb" = The "Lamp" also; "The Lamb of GOD"/ "The Lamp (Light) of GOD". See Revelation 21:23; 7:13-17 + Psalm 119:105 + St. John 1:4-9. Amen.

281. Since ELOHIM (GOD ALMIGHTYT) and Christ the Messiah (The WORD) and The HOLY SPIRIT/HOLY GHOST is ONE, whenever one worships GOD (ELOHIM) in Spirit and in Truth, they are worshipping all Three as ONE GOD (ELOHIM/CREATOR). Amen. See Revelation 7:9-12 + St. John 1:1-14; 4:24; 10:30; 14:9-11 + 1 John 5:7 (KJV). Amen.

282. Food and drink in Heaven, besides the Manna. See Revelation 7:17 + St. Matthew 26:29. Amen.

283. YAHUSHUA, the Son of YAH ELOHIM, revealed "exactly" who ELOHIM is, and how to properly worship Him. See St. John 4:24 + St. Matthew 11:27. Amen.

284. There are at least "three" correct ways to baptize someone according to Scripture: (1)In the Name of the FATHER, and of the Son, and of the HOLY GHOST/HOLY SPIRIT, see St. Matthew 28:19; (2)In the Name of JESUS Christ (which covers all three Names), see Acts 2:38; and (3)In the Name of the Lord JESUS (Let it be noted that any of JESUS' Sacred/Holy Names and Titles can be used during baptism, not just His English or Greek Names and Titles; for instance: "YAHUSUHA Messiah" or "YESHUA Messiah" can be used, which is His Hebrew Names), see Acts 19:3-5. Amen.

These other two ways must be accepted because we know not all that JESUS taught His disciples/apostles in secret; moreover, Peter was JESUS right hand man, so he would know the right way. Also, Apostle Paul was taught directly by the Lord Himself, see Galatians 1:11-12. Amen. And lastly, it must also be noted, believed, and accepted that "all" Scripture is "divinely inspired" by GOD and given by the HOLY SPIRIT of ELOHIM through holy men of EL; therefore, if it says it in Scripture, it is correct and true. Amen. See 2 Timothy 3:16-17. Amen.

285YESHUA Christ did so many things that if they were all written one by one, the whole world perhaps would not be spacious enough to contain such a massive volume of Books. See St. John 21:25. Amen.

286.We will all stand before the judgment seat of Christ (to be judged). See Romans 14:10-12 + 2 Corinthians 5:10 + St. John 5:22. Amen.

287.YHWH ELOHIM, Christ the Messiah, and the HOLY SPIRIT all taught and Commanded us to "be perfect". See Genesis 17:1 + St. Matthew 5:48 + Deuteronomy 18:13 (KJV). Amen.

288.There is a "MOST HIGH ELOHIM (GOD)", who is a "SPIRIT", and goes by many Holy and Sacred Names, including, but not limited to: "YHWH", "YAHWEH", "JEHOVAH", "EL SHADDAI", but He is still the same One and Only ELOHIM (GOD) the CREATOR. Amen. This MOST HIGH ELOHIM (GOD) is "ALMIGHTY" and Rules over all the other lesser gods and judges them. This MOST HIGH ELOHIM is the only One worthy and deserving of worship. For He alone is The CREATOR of all. Amen. See Psalms 82 (WC); 95:3 + Exodus 12:12 + St. John 4:24 + Genesis 1:1-2 (See Hebrew Bible also). Amen.

289. With a few exceptions, whenever the Word (The Holy Bible) uses all capital letters for "LORD", it is specifically speaking of the FATHER YAHWEH/JEHOVAH; and when it uses only a capital "L" with the rest of the letters lowercase, "Lord", it is specifically referring to the Son of YAHWEH/JEHOVAH, YAHUSHUA/JESUS. However, this Title is often used interchangeably for both, the FATHER and the Son, since they are "One". See St. John 10:30. Amen. For other comparable Verses, see Psalm 110:1 (and compare the rest of that chapter to Verse 1) + Revelation 19:16 (KJV) + Isaiah 7:14. Amen.

290. JESUS Christ is "The Just One" and is called that in Acts 7:52; 22:14. Amen.

291. YAHWEH/JEHOVAH our ELOHIM Himself teaches us and our children. See Jeremiah 32:33 + Isaiah 54:13. Amen.

292. The whole duty of man and woman is to "fear ELOHIM and keep His Commandments": for this is man's all. See Ecclesiastes 12:13-14. Amen.

293. Those who reject JESUS and receive not His Words, it is His Word that will judge them on the Last Day. See St. John 12:48. Amen.

294. ELOHIM's Word is "Great Power", and it is "Far-Reaching", which is another meaning for His "Arm" being "Outstretched" (although He does have Arms literally, which He Stretches Out also); and His Words never returns to Him void. For He created the universe by His Word ("Great Power and Outstretched Arm"). See Jeremiah 32:17 + Genesis 1 (WC) + Isaiah 55:11 + St. John 1:1-10. Amen.

295. For those who disagree or doubt that a "Hebrew" and a "Jew" is one and the same, see Jeremiah 34:9, where JEHOVAH Himself called a Hebrew a Jew in the same Verse. Amen. Moreover,

YAHUSHUA Messiah identified Himself as a "Jew" while on earth, and revealed that He came to save first His lost brethren and sistren of the house of "Israel"- the "Hebrew Israelites" (His Family). Also, He is a descendant of "Judah", who is a Hebrew, and a son of Israel. See St. Matthew 15:24 and St. John 4:9,22 + Hebrews 7:14. Amen.

296.The "more excellent Way" is "The Way of LOVE". See 1 Corinthians 12:31-13:13. Amen. LOVE is the greatest, because GOD is LOVE. See 1 John 4:8,16. Amen.

297.When a believer becomes One with the FATHER (HOLY SPIRIT) and the Son (JESUS Messiah), a Triangular Union is formed, a sort of "Holy Trinity". See St. John 14:20. Amen.

298.The "gathering together into one" of the children of ELOHIM was prophesied by the high priest in St. John 11:51-52. Amen. These "children of EL" are the "siblings" (brothers and sisters) of Messiah, and thus, make up the "Body of Christ". See St. Matthew 12:48-50. Amen.

299.YESHUA Messiah is the Power + the Wisdom + the Word of EL SHADDAI the MOST HIGH (ELYON). See 1 Corinthians 1:24 + St. John 1:1,14 + 1 John 5:7 (KJV). Amen.

300.When someone consistently resists EL and persists in rejecting His Truth, EL will give that person over to deception and delusion, allowing them to believe a lie. See 2 Thessalonians 2:11-12 + Jeremiah 20:7 + Romans 1:28. Amen.

301.YHWH ELOHIM (The CREATOR) has a "Heart, Mind, Body, Soul, and Spirit". Amen. See Jeremiah 30:24 + 1 Samuel 13:14 + Acts 13:22 + Leviticus 26:11-12 + 1 Corinthians 2:16 + Genesis 1:2 + 1 John 5:7 + St. John 4:24 + Ephesians 4:30 + Exodus 33:20 + Psalms 94:9. Amen.

302.He that believeth on the Son of ELOHIM has Eternal Life. See St. John 3:16,36 + 1 John 5:11-13,20. Amen.

303.The FATHER has equipped the Son (JESUS) and given Him "all" Power, Authority, and Dominion. See St. John 3:34-35 + St. Matthew 28:18. Amen.

304.The word "Principle" begins with the word "Prince", because a "principle" is a "rule", and a "prince" is a "ruler". See also Proverbs 8:14-16. Amen.

305. The revelation of Proverbs 6:15 and 29:1 is that the being "broken without remedy" is referring to an extreme misfortune which cannot be undone, such as paralysis or even death (the loss of life) for the disobedient, stubborn and stiff-necked who refuse to heed ELOHIM's fairwarnings.

306.YAHWEH is a "father" to Israel, and Epharim is His firstborn. See Jeremiah 31:9. Amen.

307.One can be baptized "for" the dead, but not in the name of the dead. See 1 Corinthians 15:29. Amen. One must be baptized according to Scripture for one's baptism to be valid. See St. Matthew 28:19 + Acts 2:38; 19:3-5. Amen.

Chapter 4:
Great Comparisons of the Holy Bible

1)Hosea 4:6 + Isaiah 5:13 (We need Knowledge!).

2) Deuteronomy 17:17 + 1 Kings 11:1-4 (It is not good to marry many wives: for they can lead a man to idolatry, turning one's heart away from the True Living GOD).

3) Isaiah 5:15 + St. Matthew 23:12 (Humility).

4) Deuteronomy 17:19-20 + Joshua 1:7-9 (Keeping the Law of EL and meditating it day and night).

5) St. John 17:3 + 6:40 + 1 John 2:25 + 5:13 (EL=Eternal Life).

6) St. Luke 10:27 + Deuteronomy 6:4-5 (The Greatest Commandment).

7) St. John 15:20 + 2 Timothy 3:12 + St. Matthew 5:10-12 (Persecution).

8) 2 Timothy 3:12 + Psalm 34:19 (Persecution + Affliction).

9) Jeremiah 20:14-15 + Job 3:1-3 (Men who cursed the day that they were born).

10) 2 Timothy 3:15 + Ephesians 2:8-9 (Grace + Faith).

11) St. John 1:51 + 3:13 (Ascending/Descending + Heaven/Earth).

12) 2 Timothy 4:8 + St. James 1:12 + St. John 5:22 + 2 Peter 3:4 (Crowns).

13) Psalms 89:29-32 + Isaiah 53:5 (Our chastisement for iniquity + Christ's chastisement for us).

14) 2 Timothy 4:8 + 1 John 2:28 + St. James 5:7-8 + 1 Peter 1:7,13 + 2 Peter 3:4-12 + 1 Thessalonians 4:13-18 + Revelation 22:7,20 (The LORD's Coming).

15) Psalms 1:3 + 23:2 + Jeremiah 31:9 (Water).

16) St. Matthew 5:34 + 25:34 (The Great King).

17) Psalms 107:19-20 + St. Matthew 8:7-17 + Isaiah 53:5 + 1 Peter 2:24 + 2 Chronicles 7:14 (Healing).

18) St. Matthew 7:23 + 25:41 (Depart from Me, ye workers of iniquity; I never knew you).

19) St. Matthew 5:6 + Psalm 107:9 (Being filled: with the HOLY GHOST, and with all good things).

20) St. Matthew 12:36-37 + 25:31-33,46 (Judgment Day).

21) Proverbs 27:1 + St. James 4:13-16 (Do not boast about tomorrow; but rather say, "if the LORD will, we shall live and do such and such").

22) Exodus 21:23-25 + St. Matthew 5:38-39 (Eye for eye [old Law] + Forgive [new Law]).

23) Psalm 107:29 + St. Matthew 8:26-27 (Calming a storm).

24) Exodus 21:33-34 + Proverbs 26:27 (Digging a pit).

25) Jeremiah 51:7-8 + Revelation 18:2-3 (Prophecy concerning Babylon).

26) Hebrews 8:12 + Ezekiel 18:21-23 (The Mercy of ELOHIM).

27) Psalm 105:4 + 2 Chronicles 7:14 (Seeking ADONAI's Face).

28) Romans 11:27 + 1 John 3:5 (The Mercy of Christ the Anointed One).

29) Psalm 124:8 + Acts 14:15 (The CREATOR and MAKER of Heaven and earth).

30) St. James 4:8 + Hebrews 10:22 (Drawing near to EL).

31) Revelation 6:14 + 2 Peter 3:5-13 + St. Matthew 24:35 (Heaven and earth shall pass away, but not the Word of the LORD).

32) 2 Peter 2:6-8 + Genesis 19 (WC) (Sodom + Gomorrah).

33) Ephesians 4:26 + Psalm 4:4 (NKJV) + St. Matthew 5:22 (When anger becomes a sin).

34) Revelation 20:12-15 + 1 Peter 3:19-20 + 2 Peter 2:5 (Judgment of the sinful dead).

35) 2 Peter 3:5-6 + Genesis 7 (The Flood).

36) 1 Timothy 6:11 + 2 Timothy 2:22 (What to follow? Follow after "righteousness", etc.).

37) Galatians 5:22-23 + 1 Timothy 6:11 + Philippians 4:8 (The Fruit of the Spirit + Meditation).

38) St. Luke 6:20-23 + St. Matthew 5:3-13 (The Beatitudes).

39) St. Luke 6:20-49 + St. Matthew 5-7 (The Sermon on the Mount).

40) St. Matthew 10:34-36 + Hebrews 4:12 (JESUS [The Word] is a Sword which searches and divides).

41) St. Luke 6:47-49 + St. James 1:22-25 (Be doers of the Word, not hearers only).

42) Hebrews 9:3,11-12 + Revelation 21:3 (The Tabernacle of ELOHIM and His Christ).

43) Habakkuk 3:4 + St. John 1:7-9 + 1 John 1:5 (ELOHIM is Light, and there is no darkness in Him at all).

44) 2 Peter 3:13 + Revelation 21:1-5, 10-14 (The New Jerusalem).

45) St. Matthew 6:2,5,16 + 2 Peter 2:13 (The reward of the unrighteous).

46) Job 33:25-26 + Isaiah 40:30-31 (YAHWEH restores our youth).

47) Exodus 1:21 + Psalm 127:1 (ADONAI builds houses: He is the Master Builder).

48) 2 Corinthians 1:3 + 1 Peter 1:3 (Blessed be JEHOVAH the FATHER).

49) St. John 4:24 + 2 Corinthians 3:17 + 1 John 5:7 (NKJV) (The LORD is a SPIRIT: The HOLY Spirit).

50) Psalm 78: 19 + 23:5 + St. Luke 1:37 (Can YHWH prepare a table in the wilderness? Yes, He can!).

51) Psalm 78:51,67 + 2 Peter 1:13-14 (Men can have Tabernacles also).

52) Psalm 78:22 + St. James 2:19 (For all beings believe that ELOHIM "exists", but not all beings believe "in" Him).

53) Psalm 78:39 + St. James 4:14 (Man's life appears for a little while and then vanishes away).

54) Psalm 34:12-17 + 1 Peter 3:10-12 (The LORD hears the prayers of the righteous).

55) Psalms 34:18 + 51:17 (ADONAI is near to the broken-hearted and those of a contrite spirit).

56) Psalm 34:19,21 + 2 Timothy 3:12 (The persecutions and afflictions of the righteous).

57) Psalm 37:23 + Proverbs 3:5-6; 21:1 (JEHOVAH leads, orders, and guides the righteous).

58) Psalm 37:24 + Proverbs 24:16 (The righteous falls seven times and rises again).

59) Proverbs 30:5 + Psalm 18:30 (The Word of the LORD is Pure + Perfect; GOD is our Shield).

60) Psalms 18:50 + 20:6 + 105:15 (The LORD YHWH saves + delivers His Anointed ones).

61) Psalm 20:9 + St. Matthew 5:35 (The Great King).

62) Psalm 21:3 + 1 Peter 5:4 + Hebrews 13:20 + 2 Timothy 4:8 (Crowns).

63) Psalms 34:7 + 91:11-12 (Angels protecting ELOHIM's people).

64) Deuteronomy 3:22 + Exodus 14:14 + Nehemiah 4:20 (YHWH ELOHIM fights for us).

65) Genesis 37:5-11 + 42:6,9 (Joseph's dream concerning his brethren and parents).

66) 1 Corinthians 12:4-11 + 1 Peter 4:10-11 (The Gifts of the Spirit).

67) Psalms 103:11-13 + St. Luke 1:50 (The mercy of EL on those who fear Him).

68) Hebrews 4:13 + Proverbs 15:3 (ELOHIM Sees all).

69) 1 John 2:29; 3:7 + 1 Peter 4:18 + St. Matthew 13:17 (The Righteous).

70) Genesis 1:26 + St. John 17:21 ("Us").

71) St. John 15:7 + Psalm 37:4 (How to receive the desires of our hearts).

72) Zechariah 3:8; 6:12 + St. John 15:1-7 + Isaiah 11:1 + Jeremiah 23:5-6 (The BRANCH).

73) St. Matthew 19:30; 20:16 + Genesis 38:27-30 (The first shall be last, and the last first).

74) Genesis 39:12-18 + Exodus 20:16 (Regarding bearing false witness).

75) Galatians 1:8-9 + 2 John 9-11 (Gospel/Doctrine of Christ).

76) St. James 1 :22 + Romans 2:13 (It is the "doers" of the Law who are justified).

77) St. Matthew 6:2, 5,16 + Proverbs 26:10 (ELOHIM rewards transgressors and hypocrites according to their transgressions and hypocrisy).

78) 2 Peter 2:22 + Proverbs 26:11 (As a dog returns to its own vomit, so does a fool to his folly).

79) St. Matthew 5:6 + St. John 7:37-39 (Those who hunger + thirst for "righteousness" shall be filled with the HOLY GHOST).

80) Genesis 1:1 + 46:2-3 (ELOHIM The CREATOR).

81) Proverbs 22:1 + Ecclesiastes 7:1 (A good name is better than great riches).

82) Romans 2:29 + Esther 8:17 (A real Jew is one "inwardly": he is a man of ELOHIM).

83) Joshua 1:7-9 + Isaiah 41:10,13 (Have no fear: for ADONAI is with us).

84) Exodus 31:12-13 + St. Matthew 5:18,26; 6:2,5,16 ("Verily" says the LORD).

85) Genesis 1:1 + Exodus 31:17 + Psalm 121:2 (YHWH ELOHIM: The CREATOR of heaven and earth).

86) 1 Corinthians 2:7-8,13 + St. James 1:5-8; 3:17 + 1 John 5:7 (The Wisdom of the HOLY SPIRIT of ELOHIM).

87) 1 Corinthians 3:23 + 11:3 (The order + chain of command).

88) Exodus 29:38-41 + St. John 1:29 (The two lambs: One physical and One Spiritual; Christ Messiah being the sacrificial Lamb of ELOHIM).

89) Ezekiel 11:19-21 + Exodus 29:45-46 + Revelation 21:7 (ELOHIM Himself will be with us and be our EL/IMMANU'EL).

90) 1 Corinthians 6:14 + Revelation 11:11-12 + St. Matthew 28:7 + Acts 1:9 (ELOHIM raised both: Christ and us).

91) 1 Corinthians 3:16-17 + 6:19 (We are the Temple of the Spirit of EL).

92) St. Luke 3:8 + 1 Peter 2:4-8 (Symbolization of stones as people).

93) St. Luke 3:9 + St. Matthew 7:16-20 + Psalm 1:3 + Isaiah 61:3 (Symbolization of trees as people-which bear either good or bad fruit),

94) St. Luke 3:11 + 2 Corinthians 9:7 + St. Matthew 5:42 (ELOHIM Loves a "cheerful giver").

95) Proverbs 3:5-6 + 4:26-27 (The right path).

96) Proverbs 4:27 + Joshua 1:7-9 (Do not turn to the right nor the left: keep on the Sraight and Narrow Path; do not go astray).

97) Proverbs 4:23 + Jeremiah 17:9 + Ezekiel 11:19-21 (The heart)

98) Proverbs 4:24; 29:20 + St. Matthew 12:36-37 + 1 Peter 2:1 (The importance of our words: for we will be judged for even such).

99) Revelation 3:3 + 2 Peter 3:10 + 1 Thessalonians 5:6 + St. Matthew 26:41 (We are to "Watch and Pray", be "sober", and "wait" on the LORD).

100) Esther 8:17 + Romans 2:29 (Who is a real "Jew"?).

101) Colossians 1:14-20 + St. John 1:1-3,10,14 + 1 John 5:7 KJV (The Oneness of GOD: The WORD is the CREATOR {ELOHIM} and JESUS Christ is The WORD and GOD {ELOHIM} is a SPIRIT, specifically "The HOLY SPIRIT"=The Three that are really ONE).

102) Exodus 23:20-13 + 32:34 + 33:2 (YHWH sending His angels before us).

103) Exodus 33:11 + Numbers 12:8 (ELOHIM spoke to Moses "Face-to-face").

104) 1 Corinthians 8:3 + Exodus 33:12-17 + 2 Timothy 2:19 (Those who Love ADONAI YAH/JAH is known by Him).

105) 1 Timothy 5:22 + 1 John 3:3 + St. James 1:27 + St. Matthew 5:8 (Keep yourself pure).

106) 1 Timothy 5:21 + St. James 3:17 (Warnings against partiality).

107) St. Luke 4:33-34 + St. James 2:19 (Even the devils believe there is a GOD).

108) St. John 12:45 + 14:7-11 (Whosoever sees YESHUA Messiah the Christ has seen the FATHER).

109) Genesis 3:1 + St. Matthew 10:16 (Serpents are "subtle and wise").

110) St. Matthew 15:22;17:18 + St. Mark 6:13; 7:29-30 + St. Luke 8:2; 13:10-17 (Satan binds).

111) Genesis 15:7 + Exodus 3:14-15 (YHWH ELOHIM reveals His Name).

112) Psalms 95:3; 145:1 + St. Matthew 5:35 (The Great King).

113) Psalm 27:8 + 2 Chronicles 7:14 + St. Matthew 5:8; 7:7-8 (Seek the Face of EL).

114) St. Matthew 7:24-25 + 16:16-18 (Receiving with faith + obeying the Words of Christ our Rock).

115) 2 Timothy 1:7 + Ephesians 4:23-24 + Genesis 1:26-27 (ELOHIM created man's spirit in His own image: a spirit of Love, power, and soundness [a sound mind]).

116) Galatians 5:6 + Romans 2:25-29 (Circumcision + Uncircumcision).

117) Galatians 5:14 + Romans 13:10 + St. Matthew 22:36-40 (LOVE fulfills the whole Law).

118) Micah 7:5 + Psalm 141:3 + Jeremiah 9:4-5 (Watch your mouth around others, even companions).

119) Isaiah 66:1 + St. Matthew 5:34-35 (Heaven is ADONAI's throne, and the earth is His footstool).

120) Isaiah 66:2 + Psalm 51:17 (ELOHIM is near to those of a contrite heart + spirit).

121) Psalm 51:17 + 69:33 (The LORD does not despise His prisoners, nor the poor, and He acknowledges the suffering of His people).

122) St. James 3:13 + Ecclesiastes 8:1 (Those who are wise…).

123) Romans 4:11-12,16-18 + Galatians 3:7 (Abraham: the father of all who have faith/the faithful).

124) Romans 4:19-22 + St. James 2:23 (Abraham's faith imputed (accounted) unto him for righteousness).

125) Romans 6:9-10 + Acts 13:34-37 (Christ died once for the sins of the world and cannot die again).

126) Isaiah 29:13 + St. Matthew 15:8-9 (Those who draw near to GOD with their mouths, but their hearts are far from Him: this behavior is called "hypocrisy").

127) Acts 7:52; 22:14 + St. Matthew 5:10-12 + 2 Timothy 3:12 (Persecution + Prophets).

128) Acts 13:30,37 + Romans 6:9-10 + 1 Peter 3:18 (Christ died and rose).

129) Ezekiel 11:19-20 + 2 Timothy 2:2 + Psalm 24:3-4 + St. Matthew 5:8 (Keep your heart pure).

130) Psalm 1:1-3 + 1 Kings 2:3 + Joshua 1:7-9 (When we are faithful and obedient to EL, we prosper).

131) Exodus 23:20 + Psalm 91:11 (EL's angels going before us).

132) Deuteronomy 10:16 + Romans 2:29 (Circumcision of the heart in the Spirit, not fleshly).

133) Deuteronomy 10:12-13 + Micah 6:8 (What the LORD requires of us).

134) Isaiah 8:13 + St. Matthew 10:28 (Our only fear + dread is ELOHIM).

135) St. Matthew 5:8 + 1 Timothy 5:22 + 2 Timothy 2:22 + 1 John 3:3 (Keep thyself pure).

136) Romans 6:23; 7:11 + Genesis 2:16-17; 3:13 (Sin deceives and causes death).

137) Revelation 21:7 + Ezekiel 11:20 (ELOHIM is our EL)

138) Micah 7:5 + Jeremiah 9:4 + Proverbs 3:5-6 (ELOHIM is the only One we can fully trust).

139) Ecclesiastes 7:1-4 + St. James 4:8-10 (Sorrow is often better than laughter; although there is a time for both).

140) Deuteronomy 31:6 + Isaiah 41:10,13,14 (Fear not! ELOHIM is our Protector).

141) St. James 2:23 + Isaiah 41:8 (Abraham is called "the Friend of ELOHIM").

142) Isaiah 43:7 + Jeremiah 15:16 + 2 Chronicles 7:14 (We who are called by YAH/EL' s Name).

143) 1 Samuel 16:7 + Jeremiah 17:10 (The heart).

144) Psalm 24:7-10 + St. Matthew 5:35 (The Great King).

145) Acts 10:39-40 + 1 Peter 2:24 (JESUS was hung on a cross made out of a tree).

146) Romans 6:8-9 + 1 John 5:13 + St. John 3:16 (Eternal Life in Christ).

147) Psalm 105:4 + 1 Chronicles 7:14 (Seeking EL's Face).

148) Proverbs 19:2 + 2 Timothy 2:15 + Hosea 4:6 (Studying + Knowledge).

149) St. James 1:18 + 1 Peter 1:23 (The Word of JEHOVAH).

150) Romans 10:9 + Philippians 2:9-11 + 1 Peter 1:21 (We are saved by grace, through faith in JESUS as the Christ and Son of GOD, and in the redeeming work of His death and resurrection).

151) St. James 1:10-11 + 1 Peter 1:24 (Flesh is as grass; like a flower, it withers).

152) Romans 13:8-10 + St. James 2:8 + 1 Peter 1:22 + St. John 3:3 + St. Matthew 5:8 (Pure LOVE).

153) St. James 1:22-25 + Romans 2:13 (Being doers of the Word, not hearers only).

154) Ezekiel 37:26-28 + Revelation 21:3,7 (ELOHIM being our EL and dwelling amongst us in His Tabernacle/Sanctuary).

155) Malachi 1:14 + St. Matthew 5:34-35 + Psalm 95: 3 (The Great King).

156) Hosea 4:6 + Malachi 2:7 (Knowledge + Priesthood).

157) Malachi 2:9 + St. James 3:17 (Do not be partial).

158) Malachi 2:10 + Genesis 1:26-27 + St. Matthew 23:9-10 (One CREATOR, FATHER, and Teacher/Master).

159) Psalm Ch. 1 (WC) + Joshua 1:7-9 + Malachi 4:4 (Blessed is the man and woman who remembers and meditates on the Law of GOD).

160) Malachi 3:1 + Exodus 23:20-23 (The Angel of the LORD going before me).

161) St. James 1:18 + 1 Peter 1:23 (The Word + will of ELOHIM).

162) St. Matthew 7:24-27 + St. James 1:22-25 (Doing the Word of Christ).

163) St. Luke 1:52 + St. James 1:9 (The lowly and humble shall be exalted).

164) St. John 1:9 + 1 John 1:5 (ELOHIM and His Son is Light).

165) St. Luke 1:53 + St. Matthew 5:6 + St. James 1:10; 5:1-6 (Being filled with the HOLY GHOST).

166) Galatians 5:1 + St. John 8:32,36 (Christ, the Son, makes us free; remain free).

167) Ephesians 4:31 + 1 Peter 2:2 (Put away from you all malice and evil speaking).

168) 1 Peter 2:4-8 + Isaiah 8:14-15 (Stone + Rock of stumbling).

169) Isaiah 8:13 + St. Matthew 10:28 (Fear ELOHIM).

170) Philippians 2:15 + Galatians 3:26 (The children of EL).

171) Philippians 2:5; 3:15-16 + 1 Corinthians 2:16 (The Mind of Christ).

172) Daniel 7:9-10 + Psalm 122:5 + Revelation 20:4,11; 21:5 (Thrones).

173) 1 Timothy 6:15 + Revelation 17:14; 19:16 (JESUS Christ is the King of kings and the Lord of lords).

174) 2 Peter 1:20-21 + Revelation 18:10 (The HOLY SPIRIT and the Spirit of Prophecy).

175) Psalm 32:8; 37:23 + Proverbs 3:5-6 + Joshua 1:7-9 (Being lead by ADONAI).

176) Acts 15:14,17 + Jeremiah 15:16 + Isaiah 43:7 + 2 Chronicles 7:14 (Those who are called by EL's Name).

177) St. John 3:34 + Colossians 1:19 (Christ has the "fullness" of JEHOVAH's SPIRIT).

178) Colossians 3:10 + 2 Timothy 3:16-17 + St. James 1:25 (Good Works).

179) 1 Timothy 1:5 + Romans 13:8-10 + Galatians 5:14 (LOVE and the Law of LOVE).

180) 1 Timothy 1:17 + Psalm 95:3 + St. Matthew 5:35 (YAHWEH the Great King).

181) Genesis 3:16 + 1 Timothy 2:15 (Women's punishment for their sins + the saving of the same).

182) Ephesians 2:5,8 + Romans 10:9-10 + Acts 2:21; 4:12; 15:11; 16:30-31 (How to be saved).

183) Isaiah 33:14 + Hebrews 12:29 (Our ELOHIM is a Consuming Fire).

184) Isaiah 43:2; 54:17 + Numbers 23:23 (The Protection of EL SHADDAI).

185) Isaiah 33:6 + Proverbs 8:12; 15:33 (Wisdom + Understanding + Knowledge).

186) Revelation 20:2 + Psalm 91:13 + Genesis 3:14-15 (The serpent, dragon, devil, Satan).

187) 1 Corinthians 6:2-3 + Revelation 20:4 (The saints shall judge the world).

188) Jude 12 + Psalm 1:3 + St. Matthew 7:15-20; 21:19 (Good fruits vs. bad fruits).

189) Romans 12:14 + St. Matthew 5:44 (Bless those who curse you).

190) St. James 1:27 + Ezekiel 22:7 (Care for the fatherless + widows).

191) St. Mark 4:17 + 1 Peter 2:8 (Those who stumble at the Word).

192) St. Mark 6:13 + Psalm 105:15 (Anointed Ones).

193) Proverbs 2:6-7 + St. James 1:5-7 (ELOHIM gives wisdom).

194) Proverbs 2:8 + Acts 9:2; 19:23 NKJV (The Way).

195) Proverbs 3:4 + St. Luke 2;52 (Finding favor, grace, good understanding with EL and men).

196) Proverbs 3:9-10 + Malachi 3:10 (Paying tithes brings blessings from ELOHIM).

197) Proverbs 3:12 + Revelation 3:19 (Christ disciplines those whom He Loves).

198) Proverbs 3:30 + St. Matthew 5:22 (Being angry without a cause is a sin).

199) Proverbs 3:34 + St. James 4:6,10 + 1 Peter 5:5-6 (Grace unto the humble).

200) St. Matthew 7:24-27 + Proverbs 4:10-12 (Wise sayings).

201) Proverbs 4:12 + Isaiah 40:31 (Running and not growing weary or stumbling).

202) Psalm 1:1 + Proverbs 4:14 (Do not follow evil).

203) Revelation 11:12 + 2 Peter 1:18 (A Voice from Heaven).

204) Revelation 11:18 + Malachi 4:2 (Those who fear YHWH ELOHIM's Name).

205) Romans 15:31 + 1 Thessalonians 2:14 (Judea).

206) St. John 14:16 + Ephesians 4:21 (JESUS is the Truth).

207) Ephesians 4:20-21 + 1 Corinthians 2:13 + 2 Corinthians 2:17 (Wisdom from the HOLY SPIRIT).

208) 1 Corinthians 14:37 + 2 Peter 3:1-2 (Divinely inspired writings of the Apostles of Christ).

209) St. Jude 21 + 1 John 1:2; 2:25; 5:11-13,20 (Eternal Life).

210) 2 Timothy 1:7 + Romans 8:15 + Acts 1:8 (The spirit that ELOHIM gave us).

211) St. John 1:1-3 + Hebrews 11:3 + Genesis 1:26-27 + Isaiah 55:11 (The Word "is" ELOHIM).

212) Habakkuk 2:4 + St. Matthew 17:20 + Hebrews 11 (WC) + Romans 10:17 (Faith).

213) 1 Timothy 6:10-12 + Hebrews 13:5 (Do not be greedy nor covetous; love not money).

214) Hebrews 13:8 + Malachi 3:6 (ELOHIM and Christ does not change: the same all ways and always and forever).

215) St. John 15:27 + 1 John 2:13-14 + Psalm 119:160 (Knowing Him that is from the beginning).

216) 1 Corinthians 2:9 + Romans 8:28 (Those who Love ELOHIM).

217) 2 Corinthians 5:21 + St. Matthew 9:20-22 (Those healed by touching the hem of JESUS' garment).

218) St. Matthew 7:6 + Exodus 22:31 (Do not give what is holy to the dogs, nor cast your pearls before swine).

219) Jude 10 + 2 Peter 2:12 (Those who are like "natural brute beasts").

220) St. Jude 11 + 2 Peter 2:15 (The way of Cain and Ba'laam is the wrong way).

221) St. Matthew 27:50-28:20 + Revelation 11:9-12 (The two prophets + YAHUSHUAS' resurrection).

222) 1 John 3:5 + 1 Timothy 3:16 (ELOHIM manifested in the Messiahs' flesh).

223) Proverbs 27:1 + St. James 4:13-15; St. Matthew 6:34 (Do not worry about tomorrow; say "if the LORD will, we shall live and do this or that").

224) 1 Corinthians 2:8 + St. James 2:1 (JESUS Christ: the Lord of glory).

225) 1 Corinthians 2:12 + 2 Timothy 1:7 + Romans 8:14 (Our spirit should be lead by GOD's SPIRIT).

226) Psalm 33:6,9 + Genesis 1:1-8 + St. John 1:1-3 (ELOHIM and His WORD created all).

227) St. Matthew 5:8 + Exodus 24:10-11 + 3 John 11 + 1 John 3:6 (Those who either saw EL or will see Him).

228) St. John 14:17; 15:26; 16:13 + 1 John 4:6; 5:6 (The Spirit of Truth).

229) Psalm 102:1-2 + 1 Peter 3:10-12 (ELOHIM watches over and hears the righteous).

230) Psalm 91:14-16 + 102:2 (ELOHIM answers us and is with us, even in our troubles).

231) St. Matthew 10:34 + Hebrews 4:12 (YESHUA Messiah, the WORD of JEHOVAH, brought the Sword that divides and separates the Truth from falsehood).

232) St. Luke 2:20 + 1 John 1:1-3 (Eyewitness testimony).

233) 1 Thessalonians 1:5-6 + 1 Peter 1:12 + 1 John 5:7 KJV (The HOLY GHOST).

234) Malachi 3:10 + 2 Corinthians 9:7 (Giving, tithes, generosity).

235) 2 Timothy 4:18 + 2 Peter 3:18 (Glory to ELOHIM and His Christ).

236) 2 Timothy 3:16-17 + Titus 1:16 + St. James 1:25 (Good works).

237) Titus 1:15 + 1 John 3:3 (Pure, being pure; Purity).

238) 2 Corinthians 3:17 + 1 Peter 2:16 + Galatians 5:1 (The Spirit of EL SHADDAI helps us remain free).

239) Hebrews 1:9 + 1 John 2:20,27 (Anointing).

240) Proverbs 15:3 + Hebrews 4:13 (ELROI Sees all).

241) Hebrews 4:16 + Ephesians 2:18 (Access to the FATHER's Presence + Throne of Grace).

242) Hebrews 4:12 + St. John 1:1 + 1 John 1:1 (The Word of YAHWEH).

243) Hebrews 5:4 + Romans 8:28 + 2 Timothy 1:9 (Called of ELOHIM).

244) Hebrews 6:10 + 1 Peter 4:11 + 2 Timothy 4:5 (Ministering).

245) 2 Timothy 2:7 + Proverbs 3:5 (Understanding).

246) Romans 3:4 + Proverbs 30:5-6 + Proverbs 14:6 (ELOHIM and His Son is the Truth).

247) Hebrews 7:14 + Isaiah 7:14 + Nehemiah 11:4-6 (The Tribe of Judah: JESUS' Tribe).

248) Hebrews 7:14 + 7:26 (JESUS Christ, our High Priest).

249) Romans 12:20 + Proverbs 25:21-22 (What to do if your enemy is hungry or thirsty).

250) Revelation 7:14; 12:11 + 1 Peter 1:19 (The Blood of Christ the Lamb of ELOHIM).

251) 2 Peter 2:4 + Revelation 12:7-9 (The angels that sinned).

252) Revelation 7:11; 19:10 + Exodus 20:1-5 + Philippians 3:3 (Worship ELOHIM only!).

253) Genesis17:1 + St. Matthew 5:48 (ELOHIM and Christ Commanded us to "Be perfect").

254) Acts 10:13-16 + St. Matthew 26:69-75 (Peters' thrice denial).

255) Psalms 4:4 + 46:10 (Be still and know that YHWH ELOHIM is GOD).

256) Psalm 107:20 + St. Matthew 8:8 (Healing by Word only).

257) Psalm 107:29 + St. Matthew 8:26-27 (ADONAI calming the storm).

258) St. Matthew 5:6 + Psalm 107:9 (The hungry and thirsty being filled).

259) Jeremiah 51:7-8 + Revelation 18:2-3 (Prophecy).

260) Psalm 105:4 + 2 Chronicles 7:14 (Seeking the LORD's Face).

261) Psalm 106:3 + St. Matthew 5:6-10 (Blessed are the righteous).

262) 2 Chronicles 7:14 + Isaiah 43:7 (Those called by EL's Name).

263) 2 Chronicles 7:14 + St. James 4:10 (Humbling ourselves).

264) Genesis 15:6 + St. James 2:23 + St. John 15:15 (The Friend of ELOHIM).

265) Deuteronomy 7:6-7 + 1 Peter 2:9-10 (A special, holy, and peculiar people unto EL).

266) 2 Chronicles 7:14 + Ezekiel 18:21-23 + Jeremiah 18:8 (Repentance + Forgiveness).

267) Jeremiah 9:4 + Micah 7:5 (Trust no one but ELOHIM).

268) Nahum 1:2 + Exodus 20:5 (ELOHIM is EL KANNA, and He will repay His enemies)).

269) St. Luke 14:26 + Revelation 12:11 (Those who do not love their lives in this world shall keep it for Eternal Life).

270) Proverbs 10:2 + 11:4 + 12:28 (Righteousness delivers from death).

271) Ephesians 1:20-23 + St. Matthew 28:18 (JESUS Christ, the Son of ELOHIM, is the most powerful).

272) St. Matthew 5:44 + Romans 12:14 (Love your enemies; bless them that curse you).

273) Romans 12:16 + Proverbs 3:7 (Be not wise in your own eyes or in your conceit).

274) Zechariah 3:1-2 + Job 1:6-12 (YHWH ELOHIM talking to Satan).

275) Deuteronomy 5:12-15 + Exodus 16:29-30; 20:8-11 (Remembering and keeping the Sabbath Day holy).

276) Jeremiah 14:17 + Isaiah 7:14 (The Virgin).

277) Romans 8:15 + 2 Timothy 1:7 (Our spirit and ELOHIM's SPIRIT).

278) 1 Peter 1:22 + St. Matthew 5:8 (A pure heart, Amen).

279) Psalm 19:11 + Deuteronomy 28:1-14 (The blessings + rewards for obedience).

280) Deuteronomy 28:13-14 + Joshua 1:7-9 (Do not turn from EL's Commandments).

281) Exodus 28:3 + St. James 3:17 (Wise-hearted and filled with the Spirit of wisdom).

282) Colossians 1:18 + 1 Corinthians 11:3 (Christ the Head).

283) Colossians 1:15-18 + Genesis 1:3 + St. John 1:7-10 + 1 John 1:5 (JESUS the Light + Firstborn).

284) Daniel 4:34 + Psalm 82:6 (The MOST HIGH).

285) Acts 17:29 + Romans 1:20 + Colossians 2:9 (The GODHEAD).

286) Acts 17:30-31; 10:42 + Romans 2:16 (ELOHIM will judge by Christ).

287) Genesis 1:1-27 + St. John 1:1-5 + 1 John 5:7 KJV (The WORD).

288) Genesis 1:3 + St. John 1:7-10 + 1 John 1:5 + Colossians 1:15 (YAHWEH and His Son is the Light; YAHUSHUA is the "Firstborn" of all creation).

289) Ezra 7:10 + 2 Timothy 2:15 + Psalm 119:45 + Deuteronomy 33:10 (Seeking to learn, apply, and teach YAHWEH's Law).

290) 1 Corinthians 6:5 + St. James 3:13 + Ecclesiastes 8:1 (Who is a wise man?).

291) Deuteronomy 18:13 + St. Matthew 5:48 (GOD and JESUS expects us to be "perfect").

292) St. Matthew 5:33-37; 23:22 + St. James 5:12 (Sware not at all).

293) St. Matthew 13:13-14 + St. Luke 24:45 (YESHUA must "open" our understanding in order for us to understand or comprehend spiritual truths (Perceive/Perception)).

294) Psalm 32:8; 37:23 + Proverbs 3:5-6 + Joshua 1:7-9 (EL leading us).

295) Exodus 31:18 + 32:16 (ELOHIM writing with His own Hand/Finger).

296) 1 Kings 2:2-4 + Joshua 1:7-9 (Be strong + courageous + obedient + proper).

297) Psalm 95:10 + Ephesians 4:30 + Hebrews 3:7 (Do not grieve the HOLY SPIRIT of EL).

298) St. Matthew 5:48 + Hebrews 10:14 ("Be perfect"; being made perfect through Sanctification).

299) Hebrews 10:18,26-27 + Jeremiah 31:34 (Once we come to the knowledge of the truth and are forgiven, there remains no more offering or sacrifice for "willful" sin, only expectation of punishment).

300) Hosea 8:1 + Jeremiah 31:31-34 + Hebrews 10:15-17 (JEHOVAH's Covenant + Words in us).

301) Jeremiah 31:22 + Isaiah 54:5 (YHWH ELOHIM is Israel's Husband).

302) Hosea 14:1-3 + Psalm 68:5 + Jeremiah 49:11 + St. James 1:27 (YHWH ELOHIM is a Father to the fatherless + Protector of widows).

303) Hosea 2:23 + 1 Peter 2:10 (Mercy from EL).

304) Hosea 7:16 + 82:6 (The MOST HIGH + princes).

305) St. John 3:11 + 1 John 5:9 (Witness).

306) St. John 3:33 + 1 John 5:20 (The True EL).

307) Psalm 89:29-32 + Isaiah 53:5 (Prophecy fulfilled/Chastisement).

308) St. Matthew 24:35 + Isaiah 51:6 (Heaven and earth shall pass away, but not the Word of ELOHIM and His Christ).

309) Psalm 119:105 + Revelation 21:23-24 + 1 John 1:5 (The FATHER is Light and the Son/"Lamb" is a "Lamp" (Light also)).

310) St. James 1:8 + 4:8 (Do not be "double-minded").

311) 1 Corinthians 3:23 + 11:3 (Divine Order).

312) Romans 10:9 + 1 John 4:15 + Philippians 2:9-11 (JESUS Christ is Lord). Amen.

313) Revelation 7:11-12 + St. John 4:24 (Worshipping the FATHER/CREATOR ELOHIM only and properly). Amen.

314) Revelation 22:4 + St. Matthew 5:8 (Seeing the Beautiful FATHER EL).

315) Genesis 6:9; 17:1 + St. Matthew 5:48 + Job 1:8; 2:3 + 2 Timothy 3:17 + St. James 3:2 + Deuteronomy 18:13 (Being perfect; perfection: both JEHOVAH and His Son the Messiah Commanded it).

316) Proverbs 2:7 + Psalms 91:4 (JESUS Christ is the Truth and a Buckler).

317) Proverbs 2:8-9 + 3:5-6 (YAHWEH straightening our paths + directing us).

318) Proverbs 2:21-22 + St. Matthew 5:5 (The upright, perfect, and meek shall inherit the land).

319) St. Luke 2:52 + Proverbs 3:3-4 (Increasing in wisdom + understanding + stature in the sight of YAH and men).

320) Proverbs 3:9-10 + Malachi 3:10 (Paying tithes [tithing 10% of total income], and freewill offerings).

321) Revelation 3:19 + Proverbs 3:11-12 + Hebrews 12:5-11 (The chastening of YHWH).

322) Proverbs 3:32 + 28:9 (Those who are abominations to the LORD).

323) Amos 3:7 + Proverbs 3:32 (JEHOVAH tells His secrets to His servants).

324) Jeremiah 17:10 + Revelation 2:23 (YAHWEH searches the hearts of men and judges them accordingly).

325) Deuteronomy 10:12-13 + Micah 6:8 (What ADONAI "requires" of us).

326) Psalm 50:12 + Deuteronomy 10:14 (The whole universe: the heavens and the earth and all that is in them, is YHWH ELOHIM's).

327) Deuteronomy 10:15 + 1 Peter 2:9-10 (ELOHIM chose us- a "special" people).

328) Romans 2:25-29 + Deuteronomy 10:16 (Circumcise your hearts; Jews are Jews "inwardly").

329) Deuteronomy 10:17-18 + Psalm 86:5; 95:3 + Revelation 17:14; 19:16 (The GOD of gods + the LORD of lords + the KING of kings + the FATHER of the fatherless is YHWH ELOHIM).

330) Deuteronomy 10:20 + St. Luke 4:8 + Exodus 20:5 + St. John 4:24 (Serving + worshipping the CREATOR YHWH ELOHIM only!).

331) St. James 4:10 + 1 Peter 5:5-6 (JEHOVAH will exalt the humble).

332) Romans 10:17 + St. Luke 11:28 + St. James 1:22 (Hearing + "doing" the Word).

333) Revelation 4:5 + Isaiah 11:2 (The Seven Spirits of ELOHIM).

334) Jeremiah 50:7 + Acts 7:52; 22:14 (JESUS Christ: "The Just One").

335) Isaiah 45:6-7 + Deuteronomy 32:39 + Hebrews 10:31 (YHWH creates good and evil; He kills and He makes alive: He is EL SHADDAI!) Amen.

336) Proverbs 8:18 + Deuteronomy 8:18 (The wealth abundance Anointing).

337) Jeremiah 32:27 + Hebrews 12:9 + Ezekiel 18:4 (All spirits, souls, and flesh belongs to YAHWEH ELOHIM).

338) 2 Samuel 22:31 + Jeremiah 32:38-39 + 1 Corinthians 12:31 + St. John 14:6 (The Way).

339) Isaiah 54:13 + Jeremiah 32:33 (YAHWEH our ELOHIM teaches us).

340) St. John 12:48 + St. Matthew 12:36-37 (Being judged for and by our words).

341) 2 Thessalonians 2:11-12 + Jeremiah 20:7 + Romans 1:28 (EL giving them up to deception).

342) St. Matthew 22:14 + 2 Peter 1:10 + 2 Thessalonians 2:13-14 + Romans 8:29-30 + Jeremiah 1:5 (Being called "and" chosen).

343) Jeremiah 20:14 + Job 3:1-10 (The two days which were cursed by men of GOD).

344) Job 30:30 + Song of Solomon 1:6 KJV + Revelation 2:18 + Daniel 10:6 (People who are described as either "black" or "dark skinned" in the Holy Bible; JESUS Himself was described as having feet like "fine brass", which is a brown color).

345) Jeremiah 31:21-22 + Isaiah 7:14; 9:6 + St. Matthew 1:20-23 + St. Luke 2:9-19 (Messages about "the Virgin" or "a Virgin"

giving birth to a man child: YAHUSHUA Messiah "IMMANU'EL" JESUS the Christ).

346) Revelation 3:21; 21:7 + St. John 3:35 + St. Matthew 28:18 (Those who overcome).

347) Romans 3:29-30 + St. James 2:19 + Isaiah 45:5-7 (There is only One GOD: YHWH ELOHIM).

348) Deuteronomy 18:13 + St. Matthew 5:48 (What YAHWEH the FATHER and YAHUSHUA the Son expects of us: perfection).

349) Revelation 1:5 + Isaiah 9:6 + Proverbs 8:14-16 (The Prince JESUS).

350) Proverbs 6:23 + Psalm 119:105 (The Word is our Lamp and Light).

351) Proverbs 6:15 + 29:1 (Consequences for not heeding ELOHIM's fairwarnings).

352) Exodus 13:21-22; 40:34 + St. Matthew 17:5 (JEHOVAH YAHWEH speaking out of a cloud).

353) St. John 16:14; 17:1-5 (The FATHER and Son glorifying One another).

354) Psalms 1:3; 23:2 + Jeremiah 31:9 (Being led by "rivers of waters").

355) Galatians 5:13 + 1 Peter 2:16 (Called to "liberty" to serve others).

356) Jeremiah 31:28 + Ecclesiastes 3:3 (A time to break down and a time to build up).

357) Jeremiah 17:10 + 21:14 (YHWH rendering to every man according to each man's doing).

358) Jeremiah 22:15-16 + St. James 1:27 (Doing justice is "knowing EL").

359) 2 Peter 2:1-3 + Jeremiah 23:14, 21-22 + St. Matthew 7:15-20 (Beware of false prophets).

360) Joshua 1:7-9 + Psalm 1 (WC) + 2 Chronicles 34:31 (Meditating on and obeying the Word).

361) Proverbs 13:7 + St. Mark 8:36 (Someone who gains the whole world but loses his own soul).

362) Proverbs 13:13 + 28:9 + 29:1 (One who despises or refuses to hear the Law/Word).

363) 2 Timothy 3:12 + Acts 9:1-5 + Galatians 1:13 (Persecution of the Saints/Church).

364) St. Matthew 16:16-17; 22:41-45 + Psalm 110:1 (Christ/Messiah: the Son of ELOHIM).

365) St. Matthew 15:18-20 + Proverbs 4:23 + Jeremiah 17:9 (The heart: purify it!).

366) Isaiah 59:18 + Deuteronomy 32:35 + Romans 12:19 + Proverbs 20:22; 25:21-22 (Vengeance is the LORD's).

367) Isaiah 40:30-31 + Job 33:25-26 (Restoration to youthfulness).

368) St. John 16:23-24 + St. Matthew 7:7-8 (Ask and ye shall receive).

369) St. John 15:6 + St. Matthew 13:41-42 + Revelation 20:15 (The evildoers will be cast into hell).

370) Jeremiah 1:5 + St. John 15:16 (It is the FATHER YHWH and His Christ who Ordains us).

371) Romans 12:2 + Romans 8:29 (Do not be conformed to this world, but to the image of Christ, the Son of YHWH).

372) Psalm 45:7-17 + Song of Solomon 7:1 (The king and prince's daughter).

373) Deuteronomy 24:1-4 + St. Matthew 5:31-32 + St. Mark 10:11-12 (Divorce/Marriage).

374) St. Matthew 5:40 + Job 1:6-12 (Being sued by evildoers).

375) Leviticus 4:35 + St. James 5:15 (Sins being forgiven).

376) 1 Peter 1:10-11 + Revelation 12:11 (Testimony/testifying).

377) Job 1:1 + Proverb 2:21 (Perfect + upright).

378) 1 Peter 5:8 + Job 1:7 (Satan walking to and fro).

379) Job 1:1,8 + Genesis 6:9 (Noah and Job are called "perfect").

380) St. Matthew 28:19 + 1 John 5:7 KJV (YHWH is a "Triune" ELOHIM, meaning 3 in 1).

381) 1 Peter 2:12 + St. Luke 19:43-44 + Isaiah 10:3 (The Day of Visitation).

382) St. Luke 19:38 + St. Matthew 5 :35 (The King).

383) St. Luke 9:1-2; 22:14 + St. Mark 6:7 (The Twelve Disciples/Apostles).

384) St. Luke 1:52 + St. James 1:9 (Exalting the lowly).

385) St. Luke 1:53 + St. James 5:1-6 (Humbling the rich).

386) Proverbs 24:23 + St. James 2:1,3,9 (Do not have respect of persons; be not partial/prejudice).

387) St. John 13:17 + St. Matthew 7:24-27 (Obeying JESUS is our Foundation).

388) Exodus 19:5-6 + 1 Peter 2:5,9-10 (Peculiar people; priests, holy nation unto YAHWEH).

389) 1 Thessalonians 5:2 + 2 Peter 3:10 (The Day of ADONAI comes as a thief in the night).

390) 1 Thessalonians 5:15 + 1 Peter 3:9 (Do not render evil for evil).

391) 1 Peter 1:18-19 + Revelation 12:11 (The Power of the Blood of the Lamb/Christ).

392) Romans 6:23 + Ezekiel 18:4 (The wages of sin is death to one's soul).

393) St. James 1:22 + Ezekiel 18:21-22 (Be "doers" of the Word/Law).

394) Ephesians 3:20 + 2 Timothy 1:7 (ELOHIM has given us a spirit of power, and of Love, and of a sound mind).

395) 1 Timothy 2:5 + Deuteronomy 6:4 (YHWH ELOHIM is ONE).

Chapter 5:
Great Promises of The Holy Bible +
Great Prayers of The Holy Bible

1)Revelation 21:7 [The Greatest Promise in the Holy Bible; it is directed to everyone who "overcomes"].

2) Revelation 3:20-21 [The second Greatest Promise in the Holy Bible, and it is like unto the first; again, it is given to those who "overcomes"].

3) Hebrews 11:6 [EL is a Rewarder of them who "diligently" seek Him].

4) St. James 1:5 [When we ask the FATHER for wisdom, He will give it to us, as long as we have faith and do not doubt].

5) 1 John 2:25; 5:11-13 + St. John 3:16-17 [The Promise of the Saviour and Eternal Life].

6) Isaiah 65:23-24 [We and our children and our descendants are blessed; YHWH ELOHIM hears us and will answer us].

7) St. John 15:7 [If we abide in Christ and His Words abide in us, we can ask Him for whatsoever we desire].

8) Psalm 37:4 [When we delight ourselves in ADONAI, He will give us the desires of our heart].

9) Isaiah 59:21 [YHWH's covenant with us: giving us His Spirit and Words].

10) Deuteronomy 28:1-14 [The Blessings for obedience].

11) Jeremiah 31(WC) and spec. Verses 1,12-14, 23-28, 31-34 [YHWH shall be our ELOHIM, and we shall not sorrow any more at all].

12) Jeremiah 33:3, 6-11 [When we call upon YAHWEH ELOHIM, He will show us "great and mighty" things which we do not know; and He will save us].

13) Revelation 21:1-5, 10-14 + 2 Peter 3:13 [The New Jerusalem].

14) Zechariah 8:3-8 [ELOHIM Himself saving us and giving us joy].

15) Isaiah 54:17 [No weapon formed against the servants of YHWH shall prosper, and every tongue that rises against us shall be condemned].

16) Deuteronomy 3:22 [Our ELOHIM will fight for us].

17) Isaiah 40:30-31 + Job 33:25-26 [Being restored to youthfulness].

18) Jeremiah 17:7 [We are blessed when we trusts in JEHOVAH and make Him our Hope].

19) St. Matthew 5:12 [Great Reward awaits us in Heaven].

20) St. Mark 13:13 [Salvation: although we will be "hated" of all men for JESUS' sake, we will be saved if we persevere and endure unto the end].

21) Romans 6:3-9 [Oneness with Messiah; thus, no more death].

22) Jeremiah 29:11-14 [ELOHIM ordained future, etc.].

23) St. Luke 2:10-11 [Good news of YESHUAS' Birth].

24) Acts 13:30-39 [The sure mercies of David: seeing no corruption, justification].

25) St. John 14:14 [Those of us who are in Christ can ask Him to do anything].

26) St. John 14:2-3 [The Messiah promises to go and "prepare" a place for us and "come again" to receive us unto Himself].

27) St. John 14:15-18 [YAHUSHUA promises to send "the Comforter", the "Spirit of Truth", who shall be "in" us and "abide" with us "forever"].

28) St. Matthew 18:19-20 [The Amazing Promise which Christ made to those who believe in His Name: when we "touch and agree" as one concerning anything we ask the FATHER in JESUS' Name, it will be established and done for us by the FATHER in heaven; and when two or three gather together in JESUS' Name, He is there in the midst (every time!)].

29) St. James 1:17 [Every good and perfect Gift comes from the FATHER above].

30) Isaiah 54:13 [All of our children shall be taught by YAHWEH Himself].

31) Jeremiah 50:20 [The great pardoning of YHWH].

32) Jeremiah 31:26 + Proverbs 3:24 [Our sleep/rest being sweet unto us].

33) St. John 16:22-24 + St. Matthew 7:7-8,11 [Ask and it shall be given us]. Amen and Amen. Shalom!

Great Prayers of The Holy Bible:

1.Christ JESUS' Prayer, the Son of GOD: St. John Chapter 17 (WC=Whole Chapter).

2. A Prayer taught by King YESHUA to His disciples: St. Matthew 6:9-13.

3. King Solomon's Prayer: 1 Kings 3:3-15.

4. Prophet Jeremiah's Prayer: Jeremiah 32:16b-25.

5. The Virgin Mary's Prayer, The Mother of the Anointed One, the Mother of the Son of GOD: St. Luke 1:46-55.

Chapter 6:
Great Blessings of The Holy Bible + How to Ensure That You Are Blessed? + The Names of the Original Twelve Disciples/Apostles of Adonai + The Reasons/Purposes for JESUS' Coming/Manifestation on Earth (See Micah 5:2):

1.Psalm Chapter 1 [WC] (Blessed is the man…).

2. Deuteronomy 28:1-14 (The Blessings for obedience).

3. St. Matthew 5:3-11 (The Blessings of JESUS Christ in the Beatitudes).

4. Jeremiah 17:7 (Blessed is the man…).

5. St. Luke 1:35; 2:10-11 (The Blessed Birth of Christ-the Saviour of the world).

6. Exodus 23:25 (Blessing of Bread + Water + Healing).

7. Malachi 3:10 (The Overflowing + Abundant Blessing of paying tithes).

How to Ensure That You Are Blessed?

To put "Insurance" on your blessings, do this:

1)First believe! Remember that ELOHIM is not a man that He shall lie; also remember that it is "impossible" to please ELOHIM without faith. Therefore, let all that you think, say, and do be done in faith. Be "faithful-full of faith". See Numbers 23:19 + Hebrews 11:6 + Romans 14:23. Amen.

2) Be that blessed man spoken of in Psalms 1. Amen.

3) Be that man or woman spoken of by Adonai in the Beatitudes (See the beginning of the Sermon on the Mount by YAHUSHUA Christ in St. Matthew 5:3-12; also, obey "all" of YAHUSHUA's Teachings and Commandments). Amen.

4) Be that obedient child of ELOHIM spoken of in Deuteronomy 28:1-14. Amen.

5) Do what Malachi 3:10 says: "pay your tithes", which means giving GOD 10% of your increase/income, by doing what GOD tells you to do with that 10%. This usually includes donations to help the poor and needy, giving to certain individuals, churches, or charities. You can even give more than 10%. This is called a "free-will offering". Thus, YAHWEH will rain His blessings upon you abundantly. Amen.

6) Delight yourself in the LORD. See Psalm 37:4. Amen.

And to put "Insurance" on your children being blessed:

7) You yourself live a righteous life of integrity as an example to them and for them (your children), and for others. See Proverbs 20:7. Amen.

The Names of the Original Twelve Disciples/Apostles of Christ:

1.Simon Peter

2. Andrew

3. James

4) James (the other)

5. John

6. Philip

7. Bartholomew

8. Thomas

9. Matthew

10. Thaddaus

11. Simon the Zealot

12. Judas Iscariot (who betrayed the Lord, and was thus subsequently replaced by Matthias).

See St. Matthew 10:1-4 + Acts 1:12-26.

The Reasons/Purposes for JESUS' Coming/Manifestation on Earth:

1)St. John 9:39 (For Judgment).

2) St. John 10:10 (To give believers "Life and Life more abundantly").

3) 1 John 3:5 (To take away our sins).

4) 1 John 3:8 (To destroy the works of the devil).

5) St. Luke 4:43 (To Preach the Kingdom of ELOHIM).

6) St. Matthew 5:17-19 (To fulfill the Law of EL).

7) 1 Peter 2:21-25 (To be our Perfect "Example" of how to live a life pleasing to the FATHER).

8) St. John 12:27 (To die for our sins and to rise for our salvation).

9) St. John 18:37 (To testify to the Truth).

10) St. John 3:16-17 (To give His faithful believers "Everlasting Life/Eternal Life"; and that He might save the world).

11) St. Matthew 18:11 (To save that which was lost).

12) Ephesians 2:16 + Colossians 1:19-22 + 2 Corinthians 5:18-19 (To "reconcile" us to the FATHER).

Chapter 7:
Names and Titles of ELOHIM (GOD/EL) + Names and Titles of The Son of ELOHIM, The Anointed One/Christ/Messiah

Names + Titles of GOD MOST HIGH, The CREATOR of all:

1)ELOHIM: GOD the CREATOR; the Living GOD.

2) YHWH: YOD HAY WAV HAY: YAHWEH: I AM THAT I AM/ I AM WHO I AM; I AM; The LORD.

3) EL SHADDAI: GOD ALMIGHTY.

4) ADONAI: My LORD; My MASTER.

5) YAHWEH-Jireh: The LORD will Provide.

6) YAHWEH-Rapha: The LORD is our Healer.

7) YAHWEH-Nissi: The LORD is my Banner.

8) YAHWEH-Mekaddesh: The LORD Who Sanctifies.

9) YAHWEH-Shalom: The LORD is Peace.

10) YAHWEH-Tsidkenu: The LORD our Righteousness.

11) YAHWEH-Rohi: The LORD is my Shepherd.

12) YAHWEH-Shamma: The LORD is There.

13) YAHWEH-Sabaoth: The LORD of Hosts (Armies).

14) YAHWEH-Selah: The LORD my Rock.

15) EL ELYON:GOD MOST HIGH.

16) EL ROI: The GOD Who Sees me.

17) EL OLAM: The Everlasting/Eternal GOD.

18) EL GIBOR: Mighty GOD.

19) ELOHAY MISHPAT: The GOD of Justice.

20) ELOHAY SELICHOT: GOD of Forgiveness.

21) ELOHAY MIKAROV: GOD Who is Near.

22) ELOHAY TEHILATI: GOD of my Praise.

23) ELOHAY YISHI: GOD of my Salvation.

24) EL HaNe'eman: the Faithful GOD.

25) IMMANU'EL: GOD with us.

26) JEHOVAH: YAHOVAH: The LORD.

27) AV/AVI/AVINU: FATHER/My FATHER/The FATHER/Our FATHER.

28) EL KANNA: JEALOUS GOD.

29) AB/ABBA: DADDY/FATHER.

30) ESH OKLAH: Consuming Fire.

31) ADONIYAH/MARYAH: LORD YAH.

32) YAHUSHUA: YESHUA: JESUS: GOD Saves; YAHWEH/JEHOVAH is Salvation.

33) The HOLY GHOST: The HOLY SPIRIT; The SPIRIT of ELOHIM. Amen and Amen.

Names + Titles of The Son of GOD:

1)YAHUSHUA Messiah: JESUS Christ; YESHUA; IMMANU'EL. (Isaiah 7:14 + St. Matthew 1:23,25 + St. Luke 1:31).

2) The True Vine (St. John 15:1).

3) A Rod (Isaiah 11:1).

4) A Branch (Isaiah 11:1).

5) The BRANCH (Zechariah 6:12).

6) The Prince of Shalom (Peace) (Isaiah 9:6).

7) Everlasting Father (Isaiah 9:6).

8) The Prince of Life (Acts 3:15).

9) The Son of the Living ELOHIM (St. Matthew 16:16-17).

10) The Son of The HIGHEST/MOST HIGH (St. Luke 1:32).

11) Apostle and High Priest (Hebrews 3:1).

12) Author and Finisher of our Faith (Hebrews 12:2).

13) The Prince of the Kings of the Earth (Revelation 1:5 KJV).

14) Wonderful Counselor (Isaiah 9:6).

15) Mighty EL (Isaiah 9:6).

16) EL SHADDAI/ The ALMIGHTY (Revelation 1:8).

17) The ALPHA and the OMEGA (Revelation 1:8).

18) The First and the Last (Revelation 1:17).

19) The Beginning and the Ending (Revelation 1:8 KJV).

20) The KING of Kings and The LORD of Lords (1 Timothy 6:15 + Revelation 17:14; 19:16).

21) Supreme King/Great King (St. Matthew 5:35 + 1 Peter 2:13 + 1 Timothy 6:15 + Revelation 17:14; 19:16).

22) Faithful and True (Revelation 19:11).

23) The Faithful Witness (Revelation 1:5).

24) The Firstborn/The Only Begotten Son of the FATHER/The First Begotten of the dead (Romans 8:29 + Colossians 1:15 + Revelation 1:5 + 1 John 5:1).

25) The Way, The Truth, and The Life (St. John 14:6).

26) The Savior of the world (1 John 4:14 + St. John 3:17).

27)The WORD of ELOHIM (Revelation 19:13 + St. John 1:1,14 + 1 John 5:7 KJV).

28) Christ the Lord (St. Luke 2:11).

29) Adonai/the Lord (St. Luke 2:11).

30) The Rose of Sharon (Song of Solomon 2:1). Amen and Amen.

Bonus Section

Why You Need to Repent Before It's Too Late:

Christ said no one knows the day nor the hour that He will return, except the FATHER. Since we do not know when the Messiah will return to judge the world (for He may appear tomorrow for all we know), so it is good to live "everyday" as if our Redeemer and Saviour will come for us tomorrow. If you have not repented, believed the Word of GOD, been baptized, and been saved, you need to make these things your top priorities and accomplish them "immediately" before it is too late. Remember, there are only two places you can go after death, resurrection, and judgment, and that is: Heaven or hell. It is "your" choice and "only you" will suffer the consequences if you choose hell. Mine brothers and sisters, choose Heaven, choose salvation, come to JESUS Christ the Messiah, the Son of the Living ELOHIM (GOD), and save your soul! Amen. (See St. Matthew 24:36-44). Amen.

I will give you some Holy Scripture Verses from the Word of our FATHER and CREATOR to start you on your new journey. Remember, no one knows the Day nor time when the JUDGE will come; there is no time to play. Fair Warning!

Before you begin studying the following Holy Scriptures, pray this prayer: "HOLY SPIRIT of the MOST HIGH Living GOD, the only GOD, I repent and I am ready to change for the better with Your help and guidance. Teach me the right way, help me to understand the Truth of Your Word, and help me to know and do Your will. In the Name of JESUS Christ the Messiah, I pray. Amen.

Here are more reasons to repent, with Scripture supporting:

2 Chronicles 7:14 "If My people who are called by My Name will humble themselves, and pray and seek My Face, and turn from their wicked ways, then will I hear from heaven, and will forgive their sin and heal their land." Amen.

Hence, this Holy Scripture Verse reveals what repentance is: (1)Humbling ourselves; (2)Praying (asking for forgiveness for past wrongs and sins); (3)Seeking the Face of our FATHER and CREATOR (in His Word-studying and doing His Word); (4)Turning from our wicked ways (turning away from all evil and wrong; start living righteous and being holy).

2 Peter 3:9 "The Lord is not slow concerning His promise (to come), as some count slowness, but is longsuffering toward us, not willing that any should perish (die in sin), but that all should come to repentance." Amen.

GOD is merciful to us, not wanting us to die in sin, but come to repentance.

2 Corinthians 7:10 "For godly sorrow produces repentance leading to salvation (Eternal Life in Heaven), not to be regretted; but worldly sorrow produces death." Amen.

Thus, there are two types of sorrow: (1) godly (sincere + righteous); (2) worldly (hypocritical + selfish). Choose the first!

St. Luke 13:3 "I (Christ) tell you, no; but unless you repent you will all likewise perish." Amen

Self-explanatory: Repent or die!

St. Mark 16:16 "He who believes and is baptized will be saved; but he who does not believe will be condemned." Amen.

Hence, we perceive that along with our repentance, we must "believe and be baptized".

Final Words: Repent, Come to GOD, Change for the better, and Live!

How to Receive the HOLY SPIRIT:

(See St. John 14:15-18,26 + Acts 2:38; 10:38 + St. Luke 11:13 + St. Matthew 28:19)

Prayer (first, say this prayer and mean it in sincerity): FATHER in Heaven, I ask forgiveness of all of my sins. I am ready to stop living for the pleasures of this world and for the lusts of men. I am ready to start living for You right now, to learn your will and do it. Use me, my FATHER and CREATOR, the LOVER of my soul. I submit and surrender to You, FATHER GOD, and to Your authority, power, and SPIRIT. I ask and invite Your Holy Son JESUS Christ into my life and into my heart to dine and dwell with me for eternity. Thank You, Heavenly FATHER MOST HIGH. In the Name of Christ JESUS, the Nazarene. Amen.

Confession: To be saved (receive Salvation), make the following confession "aloud" and believe it "in" your heart: "In accordance and in agreement with Romans 10:9-10, I confess with my mouth that JESUS Christ is Lord, and I believe in my heart that GOD raised Him from the dead." Amen.

Finally, ask and receive: Once you have sincerely repented (felt godly sorrow for committing the sins that you committed, and agreed to change and stop sinning, or do your best not to sin), and you have prayed for forgiveness and invited JESUS Christ inside you to be your personal Lord and Saviour, the next step closer to GOD is asking Him to give you His HOLY SPIRIT to be your Helper and Comforter, to assist you in living a perfect, holy, and righteous life in accordance with the will of GOD, pleasing to Him. Just ask: FATHER in heaven, will You please bless me with Your

HOLY SPIRIT to be in me and with me, to guide me, to teach me right from wrong, wisdom, the Truth, and how to perfectly do Your will in righteousness and holiness. I ask this in accordance with St. Luke 11:13 + St. Matthew 7:11 + 2 Corinthians 7:10. In the Name of JESUS Christ the Nazarene. Amen.

Final Words: After you have done your part, be patient and let GOD do His. If He don't give you His HOLY SPIRIT right then and there, He shall give Him to you at your baptism, in accordance with Acts 2:38. Amen.

"Nothing Lasts Forever" (A Poem, by: Prince Roseman):

Nothing lasts forever: may the truth be told;

if something's hot now, later it'll be cold.

Today, you may here, but tomorrow you'll be there;

yea, you may get half, but that doesn't always make it fair.

Your youth diminishes, you grow old, your body deteriorate and die;

all birds have wings, but some know not how to fly.

Life is not even eternal, unless you receive Eternal Life;

and Christ is the sole Giver of such, He's the only One who has that right.

Again, Nothing Lasts Forever, all worldly things will someday disappear;

but the Word of our Heavenly FATHER-that will always be here!

Amen and Shalom, Roseman-Lopez-Israel.

Proverbs by Prince Immanu'EL Jew'EL Roseman (Yah'El Israel), the Man of ELOHIM.

Note: Cf=Compare.

1.The wicked and treacherous speak blessings with their mouth, but their heart is full of curses. Cf. Jeremiah 9:8; Psalm 28:3; Isaiah 29:13.

2. Blessed are those who study, meditate on, and apply Mine Word, says the LORD: for a great reward awaits them. Cf. Psalm 1:1-3; Joshua 1:7-9.

3. Many are the foes of the righteous; but Justice will have its way. Cf. Proverbs 16:7; Psalm 34:19.

4. Much injustice occurs in the world: but the MOST HIGH has appointed a Day and time when not even a speck of injustice will be done to any soul; everyone will get "exactly" what they deserve. Cf. Isaiah 3:10-11; Jeremiah 17:10; Revelation 20:11-15.

5. Being grateful for one blessing brings another; appreciation for the small things brings forth greater. Yea, thankfulness to the Blesser brings many blessings, and that without sorrow. Cf. Proverbs 10:22; Psalm 37:4.

6. Desire Wisdom? Pray for it, doubting nothing; and take counsel with the wise. But he that heeds the advice of the wicked is a fool! Cf. Psalms Ch. 1; St. James 1:5-8.

7. Delighting in spiritual food is much better than delighting in physical food; and the one who delights in ELOHIM shall receive the desires of his heart. Cf. Psalm 37:4; St. John 4:34.

8. For justice' sake, ELOHIM has instilled in all created beings the knowledge of His existence; even devils and demons believe and tremble: thus, who does the so-called atheists and unbelievers think that they are deceiving, but themselves? Cf. St. James 2:19.

9. Christ, the Son of ELOHIM, is the only Way to the FATHER, and doing the will of ELOHIM, the FATHER in Heaven, is Eternal Life. Cf. St. John 14:6; 17:2-3; 1 John 2:17.

10. Not all your physical (earthly) family members are of certainty also your spiritual (heavenly) family members; for some earthly (human) relatives you may not see in heaven. Cf. Revelation 20:15; St. Matthew 7:21; 12:50.

11. Cursed is anyone who separates what EL has joined together! Cf. St. Matthew 19:6.

12. LOVE, Faith, Wisdom: these three remain; but the Greatest of these is LOVE. Cf. 1 John 4:7-21; 1 Corinthians 13 (WC).

13. Do not be deceived: a hundred baths a day does not purify one nor makes one clean: for the body itself is dirt; for the pureness of a man comes from his obedience to the Voice of EL SHADDAI and doing His will! Amen. Cf. Jeremiah 2:22; St. James 3:17.

14. Yea, the righteous come in peace, but are most definitely prepared for war. Cf. Ecclesiastes 3:8; Ephesians 6:10-20; Psalm 18:34; Exodus 14:14.

15. Practice is good and desirable to become skillful at that which one does; but it is "proper practice" that brings about perfection. Cf. St. James 3:2; St. Matthew 5:48.

16. Just as the beauty of gold surpasses that of silver, so does the Beauty of ELOHIM surpass the beauty of man; yea, the Beauty of the CREATOR far surpasses the beauty of creation: for He Himself is the CREATOR of beauty! Cf. Isaiah 33:17; Psalm 27:4; St. Matthew 5:8.

17. There are only two paths: Life and Death; choose one! Cf. Jeremiah 21:8; Deuteronomy 30:15-20; Proverbs 14:12; St. Matthew 7:13-14.

18. Those who harm children and abuse the helpless are the most despised in the Eyes of the MOST HIGH; they will receive the greater condemnation. Cf. St. Matthew 18:1-7.

19. Torturers who derive pleasure from others' pain shall receive the greater punishment. Cf. Colossians 3:25; Galatians 6:7; St. Matthew 18:7.

20. Words are powerful and are spoken by the tongue: Oh! Only if you knew the power of the tongue! Cf. Proverbs 18:21; St. James 3:2; 1 Peter 3:10.

21. The All-Seeing Eye of the MOST HIGH in the sky sees all! It penetrates, seeing through walls, grounds, and every so-called obstruction; and there is not a single place where the Eyes of YHWH EL are not. Amen. Cf. Proverbs 15:3; 1 Peter 3:12; 2 Chronicles 16:9.

22. It is worry itself that kills the worrier, not the thing that the worrier is worrying about. Moreover, by worrying you do not change anything for the better, but for the worse. Cf. St. Matthew 6:25-34; 1 Peter 5:7; Philippians 4:6-8.

23. Avoid the gossiper, backbiter, and meddler (busybody), lest you be consumed by problems that are not your own. Cf. Psalm 15:3; 1 Peter 4:15.

24. Do not befriend a meddler: for they know not how to mind their own business. Meddlers and gossipers alike cause their own destruction. Cf. 1 Peter 4:15; Proverbs 17:9,14.

25. LOVE encompasses all good qualities: therefore, LOVE is all you need. For Loving GOD, self, and others is the fulfillment of the whole Law. Cf. St. Matthew 22:37-40; St. James 2:8; Romans 13:10; Galatians 5:14.

26. Fools plot in vain

26. Fools plot in vain against YAHWEH and His chosen/Anointed ones; little do they know He will have the last laugh. Amen. Cf. Nahum 1:9; Hosea 7:15; Psalms 2:2-4; 21:11; 105:15.

27. Mine son, pray for wisdom: for in this world, you will need her. Cf. Proverbs 1:7; 2:6-12; 3:15; 8:11; 15:33; St. James 1:5-8.

28. Blessed are they that are persecuted and oppressed for doing what is right and good: for they shall reap a steadfast harvest if they endure and do not give up! Cf. St. Matthew 5:10-12; 1 Peter 1:6-7; 2:19-25; Galatians 6:9.

29. Those who LOVE ELOHIM and know and do His Word, finding pleasure in doing His will, is beyond blessed. Cf. St. James 1:22,25; Joshua 1:7-9; St. Matthew 7:24-27; Deuteronomy 28:1-14.

30. LOVE is first Pure; and there is no darkness in Light. Cf. 1 John 1:5-7; 4:7-21.

31. Generosity secures one against poverty: for the more you give when you have, the more you receive when in need. Cf. Proverbs 19:17; 1 John 3:17; 2 Corinthians 9:7.

32. Do not make a permanent decision based on a temporary emotion. Cf. Proverbs 19:2.

33. Hope inspires, and they that have faith shall realize their expectations. Cf. 1 Corinthians 13:13; 1 Peter 1:3-5; St. James 2:14-26; Hebrews 11 (WC).

34. The rich who struts by the poor and needy like a rooster, despising them, they themselves shall experience poverty and not be helped. Cf. Proverbs 21:13; St. James 4:1-6; Galatians 6:7.

35. Feed the hungry, and you yourself will be fed; give water to the thirsty, and you yourself shall not suffer thirst.

36. Now the just shall live by faith, and the words of the wise are few and powerful. Cf. Proverbs 17:27; 18:21; 2 Corinthians 5:7; Romans 10:17; Hebrews 11:1-6; St. James 3:1-17.

37. A faithful man is hard to find, much less a faithful woman! He who has a faithful and obedient wife has a rare treasure indeed. Cf. Proverbs 20:6; 18:22; Ecclesiastes 7:27-28.

38. Better is a meal of vegetables with joy and peace, than a feast of fatted cow with strife and confusion. Cf. Ecclesiastes 4:6.

39. The root of all evil is the "love of money" (greed); and covetousness and jealousy are close relatives. Cf. 1 Timothy 6:10-12; Proverbs 27:4.

40. A friend may occasionally hurt your feelings with truthful rebuke and admonition; but an enemy pretense makes you "feel" good, while all the while he awaits the opportunity to destroy you. Cf. Proverbs 27:4-6; 17:17; 18:24.

41. When the clouds darken and become heavy, they pour forth dew upon the earth; nevertheless, fire is purer than water. Cf. St. Matthew 3:11.

42. Physical training (exercise) is somewhat profitable and yields a temporary reward; but it is the work of the Spirit (Spiritual

exercise/training) which leads to overall edification and eternal salvation.

43. Mine child, eat honey: for it is good for you

43. Mine child, eat honey: for it is good for you; but consumption in excess will make you vomit. Hence, do not be greedy! Cf. Proverbs 24:13; 25:16,27.

44. It is not good that man should be alone: for this reason, ELOHIM has made a soulmate and helpmeet for each man: the Woman. Amen. Cf. Genesis 2:20-25; Proverbs 18:22.

45. As ELOHIM's children, we are to LOVE what He LOVES and hate what He hates: therefore, hate evil with a passion! Cf. 1 John 2:15-17; 5:1-2; St. James 4:4; St. Matthew 5:44; 2 Chronicles 19:2; Psalm 97:10; 119:104; Revelation 2:6,15.

46. The reward for the wicked is eternal hell fire; the reward of the godly is Eternal Life in the Paradise of Heaven. Cf. Revelation 20:10,14-15; Ch's 21 and 22.

47. Respect authority for the LORD's sake, although some rulers can be unjust and cruel. Cf. 1 Peter 2:13-17.

48. Mine children, do not throw away or waste edible food: instead, give it to the hungry; for you will be rewarded by the refreshment of their souls. Cf. Proverbs 19:17; Romans 15:30-33. Amen.

A Brief Introduction to the Religion that the Author Founded: "The UP Religion (Undefiled & Pure)".

Founder: Prince Immanu'EL Jew'EL Roseman (Antwane Duane Rosemane), Apostle of Christ and Man of ELOHIM.

Co-Founder: Angel Belloflores, Disciple of Christ and Servant of EL.

Established: December, 2024,

Mission Statement: Wake UP! Get UP! Repent! For the Kingdom of Heaven is at Hand!

Foundational Scriptures: All the Word of YHWH ELOHIM (The Holy Scriptures), and specifically St. James 1:26-27. Amen.

Saint James 1:26-27 (KJV): "26. If any man among you seem to be religious, and bridleth not his tongue, but deceiveth his own heart, this man's religion is vain. 27. Pure religion and undefiled before ELOHIM and the FATHER is this, To visit the fatherless and widows in their affliction, and to keep himself unspotted from the world." Amen.

Glory to ELOHIM! I Founded this Religion to help orphans and widows, and to teach others how to be "perfect" in the sight of the LORD, thus, keeping oneself "unspotted" or "unstained" by the world. For more info on this Religion, you can contact the Author via Email at: TheManOfELOHIM@gmail.com or PrinceRoseman777@gmail.com . Thank you and ADONAI bless you!

The Authors' Final Closing Remarks:

Shalom my brethren and sistren! It was a joy and pleasure writing this book. As the Author and Editor of this book, I accept full accountability and responsibility for any errors herein, if any are found. I must confess that even I learned a lot while writing this book. Although I always believed, as far as I can remember, that JESUS and GOD are ONE, I have come to the realization that not only are they One, but JESUS is GOD! He was GOD in the flesh. Just because GOD chose to come to earth as a Man, clothing His SPIRIT with flesh, does not make Him any less GOD. Remember GOD can do as He please. Therefore, any past statements that I may have made taking away from the "full" Deity of JESUS Christ the Messiah, disregard all those statements/comments. JESUS as GOD is worthy of worship; for when one worships GOD (ELOHIM) in Spirit and in Truth, one is worshipping the Lamb of ELOHIM (GOD) anyway, as ONE with EL, sitting on the Throne with Him. There are mainly three Holy Verses that has brought me to this conclusion, and that is: 1 Timothy 3:16 + St. John 10:30 + 14:9. And of course, the HOLY SPIRIT is GOD, because GOD is a SPIRIT and He is HOLY= HOLY SPIRIT. Amen. Hence, the Three are ONE GOD (YHWH ELOHIM EL SHADDAI). Amen.

Note: Be on the lookout for my next two upcoming Books, which shall be available online and in stores very soon: "The Will of GOD: Knowing and Doing the Will of ELOHIM", and "LOVE and the Law of LOVE: The Theology and Doctrine of Perfection". Amen.

www.ingramcontent.com/pod-product-compliance
Lightning Source LLC
Chambersburg PA
CBHW071325150726

47997CB00002B/611